The Death of
Archaeological Theory?

edited by

John Bintliff and Mark Pearce

Oxbow Boo
Oxford and Oak

Published by
Oxbow Books, Oxford

© Oxbow Books and the individual authors 2011
Reprinted 2012

ISBN 978-1-84217-446-3

This book is available direct from

Oxbow Books, Oxford, UK
(Phone: 01865-241249; Fax: 01865-794449)

and

The David Brown Book Company
PO Box 511, Oakville, CT 06779, USA
(Phone: 860-945-9329; Fax: 860-945-9468

or from our website
www.oxbowbooks.com

A CIP record for this book is available from the British Library

Library of Congress Cataloging-in-Publication Data

The death of archaeological theory? / edited by John Bintliff and Mark Pearce.
    p. cm.
Includes bibliographical references.
ISBN 978-1-84217-446-3
1. Archaeology--Philosophy. 2. Dogma. 3. Ideology. 4. Political correctness.
I. Bintliff, J. L. (John L.) II. Pearce, Mark.
CC72.D43 2011
930.1--dc23

2011031468

Printed in Great Britain by
Information Press, Eynsham, Oxfordshire

WITHDRAWN

Contents

Contributors

John Bintliff
Faculty of Archaeology, Leiden University, PO Box 9515, 2300 RA Leiden,
The Netherlands
Email: j.l.bintliff@arch.leidenuniv.nl

Kent V. Flannery
Museum of Anthropology, 1109 Geddes Avenue, University of Michigan, Ann
Arbor, MI 48109-1079, USA
Email: use joymar@umich.edu or the postal address

Alexander Gramsch
Museum Herxheim, Untere Hauptstrasse 153, D-76863 Herxheim, Germany
Email: gramsch@museum-herxheim.de

Kristian Kristiansen
Department of Historical Studies, University of Gothenburg, Box 200,
SE-405 30 Göteborg, Sweden
Email: k.kristiansen@archaeology.gu.se

Joyce Marcus
Museum of Anthropology, 1109 Geddes Avenue, University of Michigan,
Ann Arbor, MI 48109-1079, USA
Email: joymar@umich.edu

Mark Pearce
Dept of Archaeology, University of Nottingham, Nottingham NG7 2RD, UK
Email: mark.pearce@nottingham.ac.uk

Mark Pluciennik
School of Archaeology & Ancient History, University of Leicester,
University Road, Leicester LE1 7RH, UK
Email: m.pluciennik@le.ac.uk

1

Introduction

John Bintliff and Mark Pearce

In 2006, driven by an increasing dissatisfaction at the state of Archaeological Theory, despite the significance given to it in University Archaeology departments in several Western European countries, we joined forces to organize a provocative session at the Twelfth Annual Meeting of the European Association of Archaeologists in Krakow. Just as Roland Barthes had some forty years previously (1967 [1977]), challenged an unthinking orthodoxy by proposing 'The Death of the Author', questioning whether the existence of an author and their intentions get in our way in a critical encounter with a literary text, so we decided to suggest that a session on 'The Death of Archaeological Theory?' could stimulate radical questioning about its future development. We asked whether the study of past societies through their material culture – *i.e.* Archaeology – would benefit considerably by discounting the burden of somewhat dogmatic theory and ideology which has inexorably begun to obscure our pathways to reconstruct the Past over the last 25 years. Would archaeologists then also be much better off if unitary theoretical paradigms were ignored in favour of a freer application of methodologies appropriate to our real aims, which many maintain are to create as truthful a reconstruction of what happened, and why, and how life was, as we can achieve with current techniques? So we asked whether 'The Death of the Archaeological Theorist' might be a liberating thought experiment.

In the event, the speakers who volunteered or were volunteered to speak on the platform or from the floor, represented a wide spectrum of backgrounds and positions within the community concerned with

'Theory'. Some of those have given us their papers to reflect on here in this collection and their contributions reflect a range of opinions and positions; other papers were solicited to contribute to the debate. We were astounded at the interest shown in our 'provocation', and feel that this does reflect a grassroots questioning of the direction that Archaeological Theory is taking. The conference organisers also had not expected such a turnout, so the small room allotted was soon filled even for standing-room and floor-space. Nonetheless the debate was very lively and combative, with fans and detractors of certain theoretical approaches and of theory in general engaged in free-ranging and uninhibited jousting. At the end, however, came a proposal from the floor, which took all the speakers by surprise, yet soon seemed to find a wide acceptance from a large sector of the audience. It had not occurred to us, but now seems obvious and revolutionary in its implications. The proposal was simply this: why not proclaim a moratorium on the customary teaching of the history of Archaeological Theory as a sequence of paradigm shifts, one replacing and making redundant its predecessor (*viz.* Culture History, New Archaeology and then Post-processualism)? Teach rather a breadth of method and theory, in which students are encouraged to see the complementary strengths and weaknesses of all three (and other) bodies of ideas and approaches, regardless of their temporal sequence.

We shall here pick up on a few themes and remarks in the papers which follow, and give our personal take on how they relate to the session programme. John Bintliff considers that Theory in Archaeology was from the first corrupted by ideology, where individuals promoted a limited view of the world to the exclusion of other perspectives. 'Bibliographic exclusion' continues to ensure that students are indoctrinated into confusing theory with fact, by having to memorize the 'sacred texts' of particular authorities, without being encouraged to read critiques of these authors and ideas. The closure of reference systems is also referred to by Kristiansen, backed by journal analyses undertaken by his students. The process is akin to Medieval Scholasticism. Pluciennik, Gramsch and Kristiansen underline the little-explored aspect of theory traditions being driven by cultural fashions, whilst Pearce links the generational renewal of Theory to an Oedipal reaching for power by ambitious opinion-leaders in the discipline.

In reality, there does not seem to be a clearly dominant theoretical paradigm in Archaeology. Gramsch shows very well that in Central and

Eastern Europe, including Germany, not only has Anglo-American Theory had limited impact, but current discussions on the future of method and theory in these lands offer a broader view of the discipline in which older traditions are seen to form the foundation. It turns out that 'theory' was never absent or even undeveloped in many countries of this region, rather that many leading scholars preferred to operationalise models in project-contexts with a firm field and empirical grounding. It is noteworthy that this tradition of 'applied theory' significantly predates the birth of Archaeological Theory in the West, and although since the 1960s it has added elements from that direction, in essence it has been independent from Anglo-American discourse. Pearce adds that even in the heartland of Post-processualism, in the UK, archaeological departments continue to house scholars with varying approaches which cannot be categorised as 'old' culture historians or processualists, or 'young' post-processualists. In the States, the situation is different again, as Flannery and Marcus remind us. Post-processualism remains a marginal phenomenon, whilst a mix of culture history and processual approaches seems the norm, and Ecological-Darwinian insights are a major theme in much research as they have been since before the rise of New Archaeology.

Flannery and Marcus raise another key element in the debate: they provocatively query whether Archaeological Theory can be dead when it has never existed in the first place. It is surely true, that all traditions of thought in Archaeology appear to emanate from other disciplines. Perhaps only Petrie's Seriation is an independent innovation which has travelled out from Archaeology to another discipline. In the States, undoubtedly Cultural Anthropology has always been the primary source of ideas for Archaeology, an over-reliance which has now begun to lose its dialectic value with the 'loss of confidence' Anthropology has been suffering, from having too enthusiastically embraced cultural relativism. In Western Europe the early theoretical alignment by the Archaeological Theory community to a strong Scientism, followed by a U-turn to Post-modernism, was never accompanied by critical reading into these wider intellectual traditions.

Kristiansen has correlated the major shifts in Archaeological thinking to waves of cultural packages dominating Western Thought since the eighteenth-century Enlightenment. A similar approach has been taken by Sherratt (1996) and Bintliff (1993). We are indeed embedded in our Age with its own preoccupations, for which certain intellectual positions seem more appropriate than others. Kristiansen and Pluciennik predict pressure from outside Archaeology to redirect our dominant theories towards genetic and human impact theory. One is inevitably reminded of the humorous, but insightful quip of Jacquetta Hawkes (1967, 174): 'Every age has the Stonehenge it deserves – or desires'. Gramsch emphasizes that a solution to the 'Theory' crisis should be Reflexivity – asking for a deconstruction of approaches, in order to free Archaeological thinking from unquestioning commitment to dogmas arising from limited social or cultural perspectives in the present-day. We think that the discipline can go further, and this brings us to a point made by several authors – the virtues of 'eclecticism'.

There is a general and growing consensus, clearly here adumbrated by Pearce, that the reality of Archaeological Theory is that the majority of practitioners combine methods and theories taken from all current and previous traditions in the discipline. This in itself might encourage a positive judgment, that behind the Kuhnian model of paradigm replacement, as Culture Historians are consigned to the dustbin of the History of Archaeology, followed by a stratum of Processualists, *etc. etc.*, a more accurate description of Archaeology's maturing as a discipline is of continual growth through the adding-on of new insights and worktools. The earlier-mentioned proposal to jettison the Paradigm model for teaching Archaeological Theory is in tune with this rethinking. There is, as Pluciennik and Pearce point out, a tendency to belittle an Eclectic Archaeological Theory as directionless and uncritical, but this is often from a position where ideology restricts one's thinking to just one, limited reading of the Past and Present. Bintliff argues that the problem with Theory in Archaeology has been its increasing assimilation into Ideology, to which the only recourse is to return to the neutral term 'model', and this brings us likewise to a preference for eclectic arrays of methods and concepts which can be applied without *a priori* selection to archaeological case-studies, in order to bring us closer to more defensible and robust interpretations.

But is Eclectic Archaeological Theory a viable alternative to following like robots, the cultural cycles of Kristiansen? It seems to us that the answer is a resounding 'Yes!'. The growing interest in intellectually-integrative approaches to human society is one symptom, and here we think of Annales history, of biosocial approaches such as that of Tim Ingold, of Science-Humanities hybrids such as Complexity Theory or Human Cognition Studies, and the special interest of one of us in Wittgenstein's 'toolbox' approach to research. In a more practical sense, one needs only look at the fascinating way GIS studies in Archaeology have effortlessly spanned 'outsider' and 'insider' perspectives on landscapes, whilst the same can be seen in the merging of 'emic' and 'etic' in recent developments in the formal analysis of the built environment using new versions of the Space Syntax approach. Flannery and Joyce offer examples of elaborate mixes of method and theory in their two case-studies, in which one cannot neatly pigeonhole such work into traditional Kuhnian paradigms of Archaeological Thought. Nonetheless, eclecticism need not imply reductionism. Instead we would argue that combining hitherto oppositional approaches works better as complementary analyses on the same data set (Fig. 1.1).

A concluding remark is in order. Literary theorists have pointed out that Barthes' call for 'The Death of the Author' did not actually demand a complete neglect of authorial existence and intentions. Instead Barthes asked readers to contemplate the counter-intuitive alternative – creating through interaction with a text a more personalised precipitate in which the reader participates as a second author. Likewise, we do not actually demand

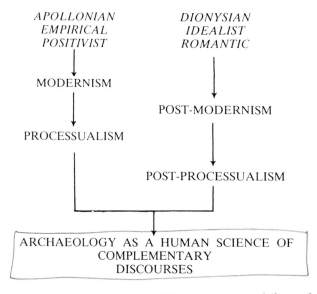

Fig. 1.1. The future of Archaeological Theory. Source: Bintliff 1993, fig 2.

the intellectual execution of leading theorists and the neglect of Theory manuals in Archaeology. In the spirit of Barthes, we do however ask that 'readers' free themselves from the imposed tyranny of a single theoretical paradigm. Reflexivity and eclecticism should be our watchwords for a future more democratic Archaeological Theory, and a healthy scepticism to being told what to read and not to read.

References

Barthes, R., 1967. The Death of the Author. *Aspen* 5–6. [Reprinted in R. Barthes, *Image, Music, Text*, 142–148. Essays selected and translated by Stephen Heath, 1977. London: Fontana Press].

Bintliff, J. L., 1993. Why Indiana Jones is smarter than the Post-Processualists. *Norwegian Archaeological Review* 26, 91–100.

Hawkes, J., 1967. God in the machine. *Antiquity* 41 (163), 174–180.

Sherratt, A., 1996. 'Settlement patterns' or 'landscape studies'? Reconciling Reason and Romance. *Archaeological Dialogues* 3, 140–159.

2

The Death of Archaeological Theory?

John Bintliff

In a famous essay (*The Death of the Author* 1967, reprinted 1977) the literary critic Roland Barthes questioned whether the existence of an author gets in our way in a critical encounter with a literary text. In the same way it is reasonable to ask whether Archaeology would benefit from discounting the burden of dogmatic theory and ideology (*cf.* Trigger 2006) which has inexorably begun to obscure our pathways to reconstruct the past over the last 25 years. Should we ask ourselves if 'The Death of the Archaeological Theorist' is a liberating thought experiment?

My thinking about ideas in Archaeology was first stimulated when I was still at school, by Glyn Daniel's television series broadcast on the BBC in the 1960s, where he set out the development of the discipline since the early Antiquarians, followed by a more *avant-garde* series featuring novel ideas from Colin Renfrew and Eric Higgs. As a BA student I was in many ways fortunate to be on the cusp of New Archaeology's emergence, being taught by what later would be termed 'Culture Historians' *and* the advocates of Processualism, whilst my early teaching years enforced engagement with the rising tide of British Post-processualism. This procession already alerted me to thinking about the reality of Thomas Kuhn's Paradigm Theory, except that the speed of Archaeological Theory's shifts of approach in his terms would mark a very immature discipline with sequent mini-paradigms. I also wanted to find out about the sources of the ideas which entered our discipline, and to that end developed a course as much for my own benefit as that of my students – 'Archaeology and Twentieth Century Thought', which was a very illuminating voyage out of our discipline for all of us. I gradually became sceptical about the 'use and discard' approach archaeological theorists were developing, not least because I was already aware that there remained much to inspire and stimulate from works written in all the major 'traditions': Gordon Childe's work from the 1930s to 1950s, for example, was a constant source of ideas for Andrew Sherratt and is still for some of my research today.

Yet of course, all disciplines hopefully progress over time in their rigour and range of tools (McNeill 1986), and nobody can deny that both New and Post-processual archaeologies have added to the intellectual armaments of earlier theorists of our subject. On the other hand, it is my personal belief, though I know it is shared by many colleagues, that each tradition has also taken much away from earlier richness of ideas and approaches to the Past. Exploring the development of Archaeology in other countries, for example for me, Germany or France, has revealed whole areas of innovative scholarship which remain largely unknown within the largely Anglophone Theory fraternity of Britain and America.

My especial target in this deliberately provocative short essay has been the overwhelmingly-negative effect of Ideological Conformity that has arisen within Archaeological Theory. The most debilitating result of what I have earlier called the New Scholasticism (Bintliff 1991a) has been the emasculation of independent, critical thinking amongst students and young researchers within the discipline. By constantly changing the goalposts, the list of required sacred texts, theory teachers have led young scholars to feel intellectually inadequate, since hardly have they scoured the pages of Lévi-Strauss so as to parrot Structuralism, than they are told this is dropped in favour of Giddens' Agency theory, and so on. Keeping up with cultural fashion, rather than bringing students to self-evaluation of intellectual approaches places power in the hands of teachers. We have found an increasing trend in classes, for students to repeat pages of leading theory texts as factual accounts of the world, making them less and less able to find their own critical voices. If one challenges students or young researchers to justify why a particular concept or approach has been taken, it is generally the case that the answer is merely that 'a leading authority wrote this'. Citation of sacred texts becomes more and more the only authority needed to prove a case-study, rather than the matching of several alternative models to the data. Published papers increasingly begin with pages of scholastic citation to works of theory, followed by applications to archaeological data which rely more on repeated reference to the favoured approach than providing convincing matching of concepts to recovered material evidence. Testing more than one reading of the data is almost never conceived of as necessary or desirable.

My viewpoint has been honed through a long series of published studies, beginning with my first Theory paper in 1979. This present article thus represents a long reflection looking back over my collected experiences of Archaeological Theory, and briefly touches on many topics already published in these book-chapters and papers in more detail than our allotted space here permits.

What, to begin with, do we mean by 'Theory' anyway? 'Theory', according to the *Chambers* Dictionary, comes from the Greek, *theoreein* 'to be a spectator, to view', and is variously defined as: 'An explanation or system of anything; an exposition of the abstract principles of a science or art; speculation as opposed to practice'. Particularly if we took the last interpretation, it could apply to the ideas of Van Däniken. So I shall choose here as a professional in the discipline of Archaeology to focus instead on 'the principles of a science or art'.

The New Archaeology formally opened an elaborate discussion on the need to set out a critique of the principles of Archaeology, and for one of its founders, David Clarke, they were to be those of Science. Here he states exactly this aim (from *Analytical Archaeology* [1968] 1978: xv):

> 'Archaeology is an undisciplined empirical discipline. A discipline lacking a scheme of systematic and ordered study based upon declared and clearly defined models and rules of procedure. It further lacks a body of central theory capable of synthesizing the general regularities within its data in such a way that the unique residuals distinguishing each particular case might be quickly isolated and easily assessed'.

Note here that he allows for interplay between the general and the particular.

And more from his pioneer ([1968] 1978) work, *Analytical Archaeology*:

'Above all else, this book is a temporary and tentative assessment of a complex theoretical development that must inevitably take one or two more generations to mature as a reasonably comprehensive and fairly viable set of disciplined procedure' (Clarke 1978, xvi).

'It follows that since one may selectively trace an infinity of particular networks through sociocultural systems and their fossil remains, no single approach can have the sole prerogative of accuracy and informative utility. Consequently, there are as many competing opinions about the proper orientation and dimensions of archaeological analysis as there are archaeologists – thus even the domain of archaeology is partitioned into the overlapping fields of vigorous rival archaeologies … Nevertheless, there is one critical subsystem within archaeological studies which…may claim *droit de seigneur* in the whole domain – and that is archaeological central theory …' (Clarke 1978, xvii).

'the aims of archaeologists vary [thus] … these differing aims … will give varying direction and potential to the analysis of archaeological data and may account for differing views of the same "facts", without necessarily invoking error on the part of any party … [This] is a strength … in that no single view … of a set of data can ever be wholly comprehensive or "true". Indeed we should encourage the analysis of archaeological problems from as many differently based approaches as possible and integrate their overall consensus' (Clarke 1978, 19).

Let us emphasise his view that generations would be needed to get Theory right as a practice, and furthermore his support for diverse approaches of equal explanatory potential … *but* the core of Theory is this:

'we may understand archaeology as having three interrelated spheres of activity … The sphere concentrating on data recovery – principally excavation, the sphere engaged in systematic description – taxonomy and classification, and finally the integrating, synthesizing study generating models, hypotheses and theories … By the continuous feedback cycle of observation, hypothesis, experiment and idealized model, the models … become more accurately adapted to the pattern of the observed data' (Clarke 1978, 12–13).

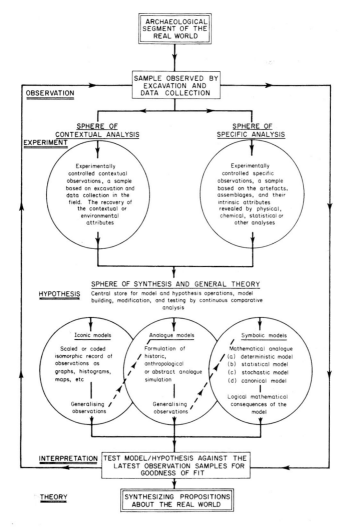

Fig. 2.1. David Clarke's model for the processing of archaeological data. Source: Clarke 1968, fig. 2.

Here is Clarke's central process for theoretical analysis: models are compared and contrasted with the changing evidence in a cycle, to sharpen and support those with the closest fit to the data (Fig. 2.1). But there is for us now, a curiosity in that diagram and further description later in his 1968 text, of this 'systems' flow of procedures: the ultimate analytical tool is to make mathematical models of the past. Here Clarke goes well beyond mere scientific method into a totally unwarranted, personal belief that human affairs are reducible to Einstein-like formulae amenable to significance tests. I have no doubt that had he lived beyond his short life this would have been dropped through greater experience with archaeological materials, but it is the first instance of a later tendency to substitute personal belief for models.

Let us turn to my next theoretical guru – Lewis Binford. (Here quoting from his pathfinding essay 'Archaeological Perspectives' out of the *New Perspectives in Archaeology* volume (1968), reprinted in *An Archaeological Perspective*, 1972):

> 'the decisions as to which characteristics are significant in the general development of culture do not derive from the data themselves; they are given meaning by the ideas we hold about the processes of cultural development. If we simply employ these ideas for interpreting archaeological remains, then no new information can be gained from the archaeological record about processes which operated in the past' (Binford 1972, 89).

> 'The position being taken here is that different kinds of phenomena are never remote; they are either accessible or they are not. "Nonmaterial" aspects of culture are accessible in direct measure with the testability of propositions being advanced about them. Propositions regarding any realm of culture – technology, social organization, psychology, philosophy, etc. – for which arguments of relevance and empirically testable hypotheses can be offered ...' (Binford 1972, 95).

Here Binford warns us that a model or viewpoint in itself does *not* add to our understanding of the Past, only the *testability* of our interpretations ensures that we gain new 'knowledge'. Yet once again, the intrusion of a personal belief – the 'worm in the bud' appears from the beginning too with Binford (1972: 100):

> 'In our search for explanations of differences and similarities in the archaeological record, our ultimate goal is the formulation of laws of cultural dynamics'.

Where did this idea of the 'Laws' of culture come from? It is actually a grand philosophical proposition, buzzing around intuitively in Binford's head in a similar vein to Clarke's personal obsession with reducing the world to mathematical formulae. Binford, who died early in 2011, not surprisingly with other New Archaeologists soon abandoned this belief and shifted his attention to testing more limited models through what came to be known as Middle Range Theory.

And now on to the founder of Post-processual Archaeology, Ian Hodder (quoting from *The Archaeological Process*, 1999):

> 'We need to break down the boundaries around the site. This is partly a matter of opening the site to a wider range of visitors and encouraging interactivity and multivocality … It is possible for new Web sites to be built which act as alternatives to "official" sites. For example, there are numerous (Web) sites at which you can find out about the (archaeological) site at Çatalhöyük. In a way, the one place that Çatalhöyük isn't is at Çatalhöyük. By this I mean that people construct their own versions of Çatalhöyük. They may do this on a Web site or in some other medium, or even just in their minds and imaginations' (Hodder 1999, 196).

> 'If the archaeological process is opened up to interactivity and multivocality, if the boundaries around the discipline, site, team and author are broken down, then it cannot any longer be adequate to separate an objective past defined by archaeologists and a subjective past defined by non-archaeologists. We all interpret the past from different perspectives …' (Hodder 1999, 200).

On the face of it, this seems a very different vision of the Archaeological Process; endless personal Pasts appear. Yet as we have now seen, David Clarke also said this, as did Binford in other texts. But at the conclusion of these passages of seeming total relativism back comes something very different:

> 'We all interpret the past from different perspectives and these different interpretations can be evaluated in relation to evidence … archaeological evidence has an "objective" materiality which limits and confronts what can be said about it …' (Hodder 1999, 200).

Now this sounds very familiar from our review of New Archaeology, but the difference here is that Hodder never states how, without a reversion to accepting a hard Scientific Method, different Pasts are actually to be tested: in practice he preaches a disintegration of Clarke and Binford's discipline with their ultimate gold standard of challenging a range of models to best fit the data available at any one time. The closest he gets is through the 'hermeneutic circle', yet as its terms suggest, the weakness of 'circularity' founded on non-empirical insights and empathy deprive such an approach of rigour or confidence in discounting other approaches.

Next to Mathew Johnson, whose (1999) textbook – *Archaeological Theory: An Introduction* – is a basic influence on the minds of the current generation of Archaeology students (quoting here however from his chapter 'Archaeology and Social Theory' in my 2004 volume *The Blackwell Companion to Archaeology*):

> 'Data do not stand, pristine, prior to theory; we cannot therefore index or measure the effect of theory on our interpretations of "the data" in a readily quantifiable way... Theory, then, does not lead to new insights in a cause-and-effect way, but it does act as a description of what is going on ...' (Johnson 2004, 105).

I see this as more slippage from any idea of 'Systematic Analysis' as demanded by Clarke or Binford – there seems to be no clear view on how ideas or models increase our knowledge of the Past.

And in more detail:

> 'theory...enables us to take the insights of one discipline and translate them into another. It enables us to show...how we might translate or modify them to reflect our own concerns' (Johnson 2004, 106).

Theory seems to be getting favoured models from somewhere else to suit 'our concerns', which appears to mean that we actively select and then transform them to our own *a priori* ideas.

> 'For some, the loss of determinacy in social theory is proof of the irrelevance of recent trends ... Of course there is no postmodern theory of state origins ..."the postmodern condition" is one in which the intellectual underpinnings of any cross-cultural

delineation of a process like "state origins" (or of "chiefdoms" or "agriculture") have been argued to be fatally flawed' (Johnson 2004, 106).

Thus never try and compare the origins, for example, of the Egyptian and Mesopotamian states (why not?). The writer assumes we are uncritical enough to allow intellectual doors to be shut in our face, it seems. We have entered the world of highly-prescriptive control of what we should think.

On to Chris Tilley, using as a testbed his 1994 book *A Phenomenology of Landscape. Places, Paths and Monuments*. Yet further slippage (see his table, reproduced as Fig. 2.2) from an analytical process of many competing models tested against an ever-enlarging body of evidence: the World of the Past *must* be looked at like *this*. Here a different sort of law-like statement, which we could sum up as – 'all pre-Modern people were…sensuous, sacred, ritual people in their essence'.

> 'The aim is to underline the affective, emotional and symbolic significance of the landscape' (Tilley 1994, 35).

this is very wrong!

infinitely open	different densities
desanctified	sanctified
control	sensuousness
surveillance/partitioning	ritualized/anthropomorphic
economic	cosmological
'useful' to act	'useful' to think
architectural forms resemble each other in 'disciplinary' space	architecture an embodiment of myth and cosmology
landscape as backdrop to action	landscape as sedimented ritual form
time linear and divorced from space	time constitutive of rhythms of social action in space-time
CAPITALIST/WESTERN SPACE	PRE-CAPITALIST/NON-WESTERN SPACE

Fig. 2.2. Tilley's global contrast between the mental world of Modern and pre-Modern societies. Source: Tilley 1994, 20–21.

'what is clear...is the symbolic, ancestral and temporal significance of the landscape. Writing about an economic "base" in relation to resource utilization or landscape use seems quite irrelevant here' (Tilley 1994, 67).

As for many models and viewpoints vying to prove their fit to the data: we are completely dislocated from any such aim. Note the dismissive 'economy is irrelevant'.

And now to a final act of slippage: Kristian Kristiansen, 'Genes versus agents', from *Archaeological Dialogues* 2004, fig. 2 (Fig. 2.3).

Faced with Stephen Shennan's (2002) proposal that Darwinism can play a role in assisting us to comprehend human actions in the Past, Kristiansen responds with this diagram to make clear to us how Culture has displaced Biology in human development over time. What is the factual basis for this diagram? None at all, this is nothing more than an artistic impression of his bare personal philosophy, masquerading as a 'chart', as if this were based on any kind of data. Here we have come to the nadir of 'Theory' if we stay with Clarke's formulation of a rigorous comparison and contrast of multiple models and approaches compared with the properties of the evidence...

All this sequence, from Hodder onwards, is not the story any more of 'Theory' in these terms. I prefer to say 'Theory has Died' – this is *Ideology* and these scholars are *Ideopraxists*:

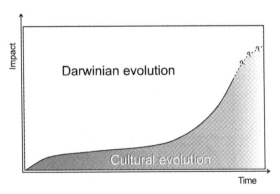

Fig. 2.3. Kristiansen's (2004) diagram displaying the decline over time of biological factors and their displacement by the cultural in human evolution. Source: Kristiansen 2004, fig. 2.

- *Ideology* from Greek: *idea* idea and *logos* discourse;
- *Ideologist* – one occupied with ideas or an idea;
- *Ideopraxist* – one who is impelled to carry out an idea.
  (*Chambers' Twentieth Century Dictionary*).

By this I mean that a central divergence occurred in the grand Archaeological Theory Project, between deploying concepts to test as structures for archaeological observations, and the insistence that structures attractive to the researcher for other reasons should be taken as the undisputed basis for organising those data into meaningful patterns. And yet I would be the first to admit that the seeds of this undoing of the Project of Theory were present in those higher claims of Clarke and Binford to explain the World through formulae or scientific laws.

Can we rescue Clarke's overall Project? In 1982 theoretical Geographers were able to elaborate beyond Clarke's basic vision, through this diagram (Fig. 2.4), which appears to incorporate Modernism, Post-modernism

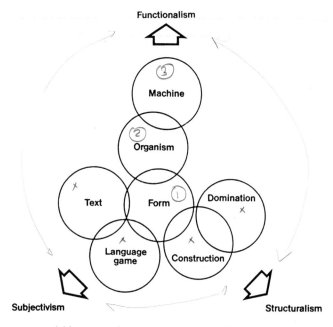

Fig. 2.4. A model by geographers suggesting a series of complementary approaches available for their discipline. Source: Harrison & Livingstone 1982, fig. 1.4.

and Darwinism, and much else, making clear that a healthy core Theory should combine insights and models from seemingly contrasted intellectual and methodological positions.

I have previously argued for a similar, Wittgensteinian 'toolbox' methology – deploying several, equally-valid approaches to probe the complex structure of past life, rather than through one preferred *ideological* package (see also Mark Pearce's paper in this collection on the non-problem of incommensurability). Wittgenstein (Bintliff 2000) suggested that human society lives through a series of forms of behaviour and kinds of discourse which are unique and not cross-translatable. The texture of human life is woven from their complex intermeshing in historic scenarios. As historians-archaeologists we can only rescue the complexity of that Past through an equally multi-faceted set of approaches, which at times are each taken (incorrectly) as in themselves almost sufficient for that task (Fig. 2.5).

[handwritten marginalia: ETHIC / ESTHETIC / ASCETIC / I love this theory]

MAJOR ARCHAEOLOGICAL DISCOURSES

CULTURALIST DISCOURSE

POLITICAL DISCOURSE

FUNCTIONALIST DISCOURSE

SCIENCE DISCOURSE

BIOLOGICAL DISCOURSE

RELIGIOUS DISCOURSE

Fig. 2.5. A complementary set of approaches for Archaeological interpretation, based on Wittgenstein's Toolbox concept. Source: Bintliff 2008, fig. 10.2.

Reliance on a personal dogma, on an *a priori* claim that 'the world works like this', surely impoverishes the researcher's ability to discover how the Past was created, since alternative approaches or insights are from the first ruled out of the investigation. I frankly confess that I do not know what happened in the Past when I start a new regional project: I might in the end propose explanations similar to what others had suspected before, or something none of us had imagined. When

I read the (usually lengthy) introductory chapters to studies heavy in Theory, what strikes me is that the analytical apparatus being set out is not based on empirical studies or experimental evidence, but on the author's philosophical or political preferences. Once the desired 'ways of seeing the world' are set out, the remainder of the study is concerned to decorate these models with suitable archaeological data. Since in reality we cannot claim such sure knowledge of the Past, it is more than desirable to bring to its remains a range of approaches, and find all the means possible to compare their possible role in explanations of our data. Stressing this inclusive and complex methodology rather than the one-dimensional limitations of personalised dogmas has led some of us to explore the broad spectrum deployed by the French *Annaliste* historians (Fig. 2.6), where all conceivable facets of human history are fruitfully reconciled in a single holistic approach: TOTAL HISTORY

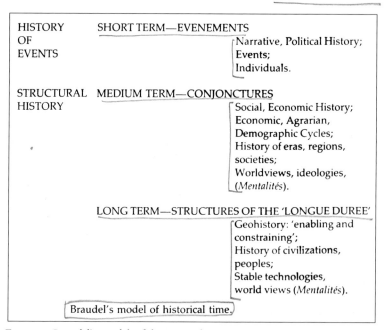

HISTORY OF EVENTS	SHORT TERM—EVENEMENTS	Narrative, Political History; Events; Individuals.
STRUCTURAL HISTORY	MEDIUM TERM—CONJONCTURES	Social, Economic History; Economic, Agrarian, Demographic Cycles; History of eras, regions, societies; Worldviews, ideologies, (*Mentalités*).
	LONG TERM—STRUCTURES OF THE 'LONGUE DUREE'	Geohistory: 'enabling and constraining'; History of civilizations, peoples; Stable technologies, world views (*Mentalités*).

Braudel's model of historical time.

Fig. 2.6. Braudel's model of history, where processes operating at different timescales interact to create unique historical sequences. Source: Bintliff 1991b, fig. 1.2.

The wide-ranging eclecticism of the *Annaliste* historians finds equal necessity in probing individual human Agency as in the pressures of physical geography over millennia, in materialism as in art and mentalities, allowing for example Darwinists, Marxists, Descartian individualists, object or text focussed researchers all to find their approach incorporated, yet into a grander, more flexible scheme of historical analysis (*cf.* Bintliff 2004a).

But let us not lose sight of the crucial warning of Clarke and Binford: first bring in a broad range of explanatory models – but the heart of their Theory Machine lies in the next, essential stage – the skillful comparison of each with the properties of the archaeological data.

In trying to sharpen my comprehension of our encounter with the evidence, I have found (Bintliff 2004b) the early 20th century debate between the great Physicists Max Planck and Ernst Mach very enlightening – *Grand Theory versus Scientific Empirical Discovery* (see Steve Fuller 2000). For Planck, an elite of very brainy ideas-people set tasks for practical researchers and then told them what they had found, whilst for Mach the best science was democratic and arose from the physical skill and high craftsmanship of experimenters finding practical patterning in real-world, hands-on encounters with matter. Mach referred to Psychophysics – the reinforcing pleasure we get from manipulation and probing of the physical world. E. O. Wilson (1984) and John Barrow (1995) explain human pleasure in Landscape with their Agrophilia and Biophilia hypotheses. Human beings receive chemical gratification which makes us feel good when we do things that have become inbuilt survival skills. We developed for millions of years as expert foragers in open landscapes and we hence needed to note and explore the changing properties of the natural environment essential for obtaining food and avoiding dangers.

I would like to free Archaeologists from 'Ideopraxists', or those who preach that a (any?) single approach or model is right to the exclusion of all others, who tell them what to think, and what not to think. Better surely to fill your brains with all the possible models and methods for your research case-study, then search for the fit between idea and patterns in past material culture in a more intuitive way; next lay out the way things now appear to make sense, but explicitly, as Clarke demanded. I prefer this way round, because research into our brain

*Multidisciplinary & Multiapproach? Yes! But make it
really happen!*

structure indicates that our non-conscious intelligence is a good deal
smarter than our conscious intelligence. Once that smart internal mind
brings out suggestive fits of ideas to evidence, then comes the time to
make a conscious elaboration of the case for a preferred explanation,
preferably with many different factors involved.

*→ International framework for Archaeological Theory → Total
Archaeology → look at International Projects and
their social/
political/
economic-
mical
influence*

References

Barrow, J., 1995. *The Artful Universe.* Oxford: Oxford University Press.

Barthes, R., 1967. The Death of the Author. *Aspen* 5–6. [Reprinted in R. Barthes,
    Image, Music, Text, 142–148. Essays selected and translated by Stephen Heath,
    1977. London: Fontana Press].

Binford, L. R., 1968. Archaeological perspectives. In S. R. Binford & L. R.
    Binford (eds), *New Perspectives in Archaeology*, 5–32. Chicago: Aldine Press.

Binford, L. R., 1972. *An Archaeological Perspective.* New York & London:
    Seminar Press.

Bintliff, J. L., 1991a. Post-modernism, rhetoric and scholasticism at TAG: the
    current state of British archaeological theory. *Antiquity* 65, 274–278.

Bintliff, J. L., 1991b. The contribution of an *Annaliste*/structural history
    approach to archaeology. In J. L. Bintliff (ed.), *The* Annales *School and
    Archaeology*, 1–33. London: Leicester University Press.

Bintliff, J. L., 2000. Archaeology and the philosophy of Wittgenstein. In
    C. Holtorf & H. Karlsson (eds), *Philosophy and Archaeological Practice.
    Perspectives for the 21st Century*, 153–172. Goteborg: Bricoleur Press.

Bintliff, J. L., 2004a. Time, structure and agency: The Annales, emergent
    complexity, and archaeology. In J. L. Bintliff (ed.), *A Companion to
    Archaeology*, 174–194. London & New York: Blackwell.

Bintliff, J., 2004b. Experiencing archaeological fieldwork. In J. Bintliff (ed.), *A
    Companion to Archaeology*, 397–405. London & New York: Blackwell.

Bintliff, J. L., 2008. Chapter 10. History and Continental Approaches. In
    R. A. Bentley, H. D. G. Maschner & C. Chippindale (eds), *Handbook of
    Archaeological Theories*, 147–164. Lanham (NY): Altamira Press.

Chambers' Twentieth Century Dictionary. Edited by A. M. MacDonald.
    Edinburgh: W. R. Chambers Ltd, 1972.

Clarke, D. L., 1968 [revised edition 1978]). *Analytical Archaeology.* London:
    Methuen.

Fuller, S., 2000. *Thomas Kuhn. A Philosophical History for Our Times.* Chicago:
    University of Chicago Press.

Harrison, R. T. & Livingstone, D. N., 1982. Understanding in Geography:
    Structuring the Subjective. In D. T. Herbert & R. J. Johnston (eds),
    Geography and the Urban Environment, 1–39. Chichester: John Wiley.

Hodder, I., 1999. *The Archaeological Process. An Introduction.* London: Blackwell.

Johnson, M., 1999. *Archaeological Theory: An Introduction.* Oxford: Blackwell.

Johnson, M., 2004. Archaeology and social theory. In J. Bintliff (ed.), *A Companion to Archaeology*, 92–109. London: Blackwell.

Kristiansen, K., 2004. Genes versus agents: A discussion of widening theoretical gaps in archaeology. *Archaeological Dialogues* 11(2), 77–132.

McNeill, W. H., 1986. Mythistory, or Truth, Myth, History, and Historians. *American Historical Review* 91, 1–10.

Shennan, S., 2002. *Genes, Memes and Human History: Darwinian archaeology and cultural evolution.* London: Thames & Hudson.

Tilley, C., 1994. *A Phenomenology of Landscape. Places, Paths and Monuments.* Oxford: Berg.

Trigger, B. G., 2006. *A History of Archaeological Thought.* Second edition. Cambridge: Cambridge University Press.

Wilson, E. O., 1984. *Biophilia.* Cambridge (MA): Harvard University Press.

3

A New World Perspective on the 'Death' of Archaeological Theory

Kent V. Flannery and Joyce Marcus

Is it really the case that theory has died, or simply that Post-modernism will be the death of archaeology?

We agree with Bintliff that Post-modernism is, for many of its practitioners, an ideology – sometimes even a kind of intolerant 'political correctness', a phenomenon with which we Americans are familiar (Flannery 2006). But the debate between Max Planck and Ernst Mach, as summarised by Bintliff, is relevant to Processualists and Post-processualists alike. From 1960 onward, we have witnessed the emergence of archaeologists who resemble Planck's 'elite of very brainy ideas-people who set tasks for practical researchers and then tell them what they have found'. Among them are individuals who feel that their role is to 'set the agenda' for other archaeologists (Yoffee & Sherratt 1993). Unfortunately, many of the would-be agenda-setters are people who do no archaeological fieldwork of their own, denying themselves the feedback between empirical data and theory that survey and excavation encourage.

So please, please, give us democratic disciples of Mach, for whom the best archaeology arises from the 'high craftsmanship' of field archaeologists 'finding practical patterning in real world, hands-on encounters' with real archaeological sites. Good site reports are the Rolls-Royces of archaeological publication. Volumes like Clark's (1954) report on Star Carr and Moore, Hillman and Legge's (2000) report on Abu

Hureyra speak not only to the authors' theoretical concerns, but also to the concerns of other scholars with different theoretical perspectives.

At the philosophical level of Planck and Mach, there may appear to be little difference between Old World and New World archaeologists. But New World archaeologists were told, half a century ago, that 'American archaeology stands in a particularly close and, so far as theory is concerned, dependent relationship to anthropology' (Willey & Phillips 1958, 1). For us, therefore, archaeological theory cannot have died, because archaeological theory never really existed. Archaeology is a set of methods; its theory is on loan from anthropology, sociology, political science, economics, ecology, biology, evolution, or some other adjunct field.

Just as the study of living animals helps one interpret the remains of fossil vertebrates, so the study of living human societies helps one interpret the remains of past societies. Fortunately, there exists in our libraries a staggering inventory of ethnographic studies of living peoples. Many of these studies refute the notion that 'economy is irrelevant' and that 'all pre-modern people were ... sensuous, sacred, ritual people in their essence', as well as other reductionist positions on cultural diversity.

Like proper followers of Mach, we believe that a good practical example is better than a sterile theorem. Let us therefore describe two under-known cases where the feedback between archaeology and anthropology has proven to be informative and mutually reinforcing.

The rise of segmentary society and the origin of war

The origin of war has long been one of the important theoretical issues facing anthropologists. War is well documented in states and empires, but tracing its origins back to earlier, simpler societies has proven to be challenging.

Anthropologist Raymond C. Kelly, himself an eyewitness to intergroup raiding in New Guinea, pored over the data of dozens of pre-state societies in an effort to determine how intergroup violence began (Kelly 2000). Some hunter-gatherers and egalitarian horticulturalists (such as the !Kung and Mbuti of Africa, the Semai of Malaysia, the Copper Eskimo, and the Siriono of Bolivia) seemed to Kelly to be truly warless; they might have individual homicides, but group-on-group violence was rare. Other societies (such as the Andaman Islanders, the Comanche and Chiricahua Apache, and the Xavante and Nambicuara of Brazil) had frequent intergroup raiding.

Kelly found that most warless societies were *unsegmented*; that is, they showed little tendency to form permanent social units larger than the extended family. Individual homicides were punished at the family level, often through payments to the victim's kin. The big change came with societies large enough to be divided into opposable segments, such as matrilineal, patrilineal, or ancestor-based descent groups. Such segments developed a corporate or group mentality, displaying a principle Kelly called *social substitution*. With this principle in place, the killing (or even insulting) of any member of one's segment was considered a group offence, and could be avenged by killing any member (or members) of the offender's group. Intervillage raiding thus began not as a pathology, but as a form of *social action*, and eventually escalated to war as societies grew in scale and complexity (Flannery & Marcus 2003).

While searching for prehistoric examples to test his theoretical model, Kelly encountered Fred Wendorf's report on Jebel Sahaba, a Late Palaeolithic cemetery near Wadi Halfa, Sudan, only a kilometre east of the Nile River (Wendorf 1968). The cemetery dated to at least 15,000 years ago, and closer to 24,000 years if the radiocarbon dates are calibrated. This was a time of hunting and gathering which long preceded the rise of agriculture in the Nile Valley.

The most remarkable aspect of Jebel Sahaba was the fact that half the 58 individuals interred there – men, women, and children – had died violently, apparently the victims of one or more massacres. Twenty-four of the skeletons were associated with 116 flint artefacts, most of them projectile elements that had entered the body and in some cases were embedded in bones. One middle-aged man had been riddled by 19 flints, striking his pelvis, neck vertebrae, forearm, leg, and skull. One young woman had been riddled with 21 flints, including 3 likely barbs from a spear that had entered her face and reached the back of the skull. A pair of men buried together had 27 flints embedded in or resting against their skeletons; a group of two adults and a child had projectile points in the lower thoracic area. Moreover, some skeletons had old healed injuries, such as forearm parry fractures and broken collar bones, suggesting that violence had been endemic.

Kelly instantly recognized this type of homicide as 'pincushioning', a behaviour in which dead or dying enemies are riddled with projectiles. That, plus the fact that women and children were included, signalled to Kelly that there had been one or more ambushes by hostile neighbours. Such ambushes differ from formal confrontations in which male warriors stand at a distance and hurl spears at each other (Kelly 2000, 148–52).

The study of Jebel Sahaba, however, did not end there. After reading Kelly's book, Fred Wendorf, the original excavator of the cemetery, joined with his collaborator Romuald Schild to publish two reanalyses (Wendorf & Schild 2001–2003; 2004). Wendorf and Schild point out that during the Late Palaeolithic (1) the Wadi Halfa area was the scene of multiple (and possibly ethnically diverse) groups of hunters and gatherers, and (2) the deserts to either side of the Nile made its floodplain and embayments a strongly circumscribed environment, one from which people were reluctant to move when other groups encroached. Food would have been abundant in the Nile embayments in summer, autumn, and early winter; but from late winter until the summer floods, food supplies would have declined and competition for them may have been intense, leading to the 'pincushioning' of rivals.

To this we would add the following: based on Kelly's model, we can surmise that the Late Palaeolithic societies of the Wadi Halfa area had become segmented and followed the principle of social substitution, which made any member of a rival group fair game for revenge – even women and children. The existence of cemeteries reinforces our suspicion that the dead were now treated as members of a corporate group or social segment, in contrast to earlier periods when burials tended to be rare and individual. An interesting aspect of this period is that no villages contemporary with Jebel Sahaba have been found, only short-term camps. Thus, at least for this part of the Nile Valley, cemeteries had preceded villages.

The Jebel Sahaba story is one of productive feedback between archaeologists and social anthropologists. Social anthropology, with its rich detail unavailable to prehistorians, provided the theory. Archaeology provided the test case, time depth, and – thanks to Wendorf and Schild's work – an ecological context: the great river's stands of sedge and club-rush tubers, catfish, Nile perch, and migratory waterfowl made its prime embayments worth fighting for. Academic dialogue has helped us better understand the conditions under which intergroup violence arose.

The evolution of Tikopia society

In 1929 Raymond Firth, a young anthropologist from New Zealand, arrived on the Polynesian island of Tikopia. Seven years later he published an ethnography which has come to be regarded as a classic (Firth 1936). Among other things, Firth's description of the *ariki*, or hereditary chief, whose authority transcended his own village and encompassed a group of satellite communities, served as an early model for how many rank-based societies operated.

Firth went on to write several more books on economy, religion, and society in Tikopia. In one of those works, Firth (1961) collected from the chiefly Taumako clan an oral history that stretched back 12 generations before 1929. In it, the *ariki* of Taumako claimed descent from a chiefly ancestor who arrived by boat from Tonga, an island noted for its high levels of hereditary inequality. Based on its adaptation to the island, Firth proposed (but had no way to prove) that Tikopia's population must have arrived much longer ago than that. If only there were archaeological data to prove it.

And now there are. Responding to Firth's challenge, archaeologist Patrick Kirch and ethnobotanist Douglas Yen arrived on Tikopia in 1977 to investigate the island's past. They found that Tikopia had been colonised by at least 900 BC. Occupation began on the calcareous southwestern lowlands of the island and spread inland to the shores of Te Roto, a body of water that would originally have been a saltwater bay surrounded by volcanic hills (Kirch & Yen 1982).

Pristine Tikopia provided its early colonists with sea turtles, abundant molluscs, and a fowl-like bird called a megapode. The colonists brought with them domestic pigs and chickens, and as their settlements grew, they doomed the megapode to extinction and reduced the supply of turtles and molluscs. They fished, raised coconuts, and made 'peelers' of marine shell that seem appropriate for use on taro, yams, or breadfruit. By AD 1000 Tikopia's forests were shrinking, domestic pigs were increasing, and wild resources were in serious decline.

Through these early stages of Tikopia's history, many of its trade goods

– obsidian, chert, and metavolcanic adzes among them – could be traced to Melanesian islands to the west. All this began to change between AD 1200 and 1600, as Melanesian exotics diminished and trade goods from the east appeared. Included among the latter were Polynesian artefacts such as basalt adzes and pearl-shell trolling-lure points; finally, after AD 1400, Tikopians began to build cut-and-dressed stone masonry buildings of Tongan type. These data reinforce the Taumako clan's oral histories of chiefly Tongans arriving in Tikopia, and strengthen Firth's (1961, 165) theory that 'the framework of modern Tikopia social structure was built up in the 15th and 16th centuries, perhaps under the galvanizing influence of immigrants from overseas' (Kirch & Yen 1982, 341–43).

Tikopia's sociopolitical changes were accompanied by human-induced environmental changes and new economic strategies. As more and more wild species vanished from the archaeological record, Kirch and Yen saw an increase in the type of pit used today as a silo for storing breadfruit; meanwhile, Te Roto evolved from a saltwater bay to the brackish lake it had been when Firth arrived. Firth's Tikopia, in other words, was the product of a 3000-year history of changes in environment, land use, trade, inter-island migration, and the responses of human agents.

Returning to Bintliff's polemic, we see that the Tikopia case is amenable to the Braudel model he favours. Firth supplied the political history appropriate for the 'short term'; Kirch and Yen supplied both the 'long term' history of the island and its 'medium term' demographic, agrarian, and economic cycles. But there is yet another lesson to be learned here.

The accounts of the Taumako clan qualify as 'memory' (as in 'cultural memory'), one of the post-modernists' favourite buzzwords. Anthropological archaeologists, of course, have long called such accounts 'ethnohistory', and they have been using them in regions like Mesoamerica and the Andes for more than a century. Just as the Taumako clan of Tikopia had its oral history (or 'memory') of 12 chiefly generations, the Inka had their memory of 10 or 12 rulers, and the Aztec had their memory of 10 or more. The conquering Spaniards dutifully recorded these histories, some of which were purely oral and some of which were kept in pictorial manuscripts called *codices* (*e.g.*, Caso 1964; Smith 1973; Marcus 1992; Jansen & Pérez Jiménez 2000). As the codices show, however, not all cultural memory is accurate: codices often are palimpsests in which superimposed layers of whitewash cover up earlier versions of events. Such codices have been resurfaced and repainted with the deliberate intent of rewriting history. 'Memory', therefore, may not only fail but can actually be falsified. It took Kirch and Yen's empirical archaeological data to confirm the cultural memory recorded by Firth.

Memorial service

It is because of collaborations like those of Tikopia and Jebel Sahaba that American archaeologists do not foresee the death of a genuinely *archaeological* theory. For us, virtually all our theory is borrowed. Nor do we foresee the death of field archaeology, since the empirical data of the past constitute an archive that will outlast any and all theoretical fads.

For us, the real catastrophe would be the death of *anthropological* theory, an event no one in Firth's day would have foreseen. We mention this possibility because some anthropology today has become decidedly antiscientific, rejecting not only (1) the controlled comparison and contrast of cultures, but also (2) the use of generalisation, both of which are crucial to theories and models. Sadly, many anthropologists who admire Braudel do not realize that without scientific archaeology, in many parts of the world the *longue durée* will always be invisible. But do not despair. Only if Post-modernism were to endure forever – which we do not expect – will there be cause for a memorial service.

References

Caso, A., 1964. *Interpretation of the Codex Selden 3135 (A.2) – Interpretación del Códice Selden 3135 (A.2)*. Mexico City: Sociedad Mexicana de Antropología.

Clark, J. G. D., 1954. *Excavations at Star Carr: an early Mesolithic site at Seamer near Scarborough, Yorkshire*. Cambridge: Cambridge University Press.

Firth, R., 1936. *We, the Tikopia*. London: Allen and Unwin.

Firth, R., 1961. *History and Traditions of Tikopia*. Wellington (NZ): Memoirs of the Polynesian Society 33.

Flannery, K. V., 2006. On the resilience of Anthropological Archaeology. *Annual Review of Anthropology* 35, 1–13.

Flannery, K. V. & Marcus, J., 2003. The origin of war: new ^{14}C dates from ancient Mexico. *Proceedings of the National Academy of Sciences* 100(20): 11801–805.

Jansen, M. E. R. G. N. & Pérez Jiménez, G. A., 2000. *La Dinastía de Añute: Historia, Literatura e Ideología de un Reino Mixteco.* Leiden: CNWS.

Kelly, R. C., 2000. *Warless Societies and the Origin of War.* Ann Arbor (MI): University of Michigan Press.

Kirch, P. V. & Yen, D. E., 1982. *Tikopia: The Prehistory and Ecology of a Polynesian Outlier.* Bernice P. Bishop Museum Bulletin 238. Honolulu: Bishop Museum Press.

Marcus, J., 1992. *Mesoamerican Writing Systems: Propaganda, Myth, and History in Four Ancient Civilizations.* Princeton (NJ): Princeton University Press.

Moore, A. M. T., Hillman, G. C. & Legge, A. J., 2000. *Village on the Euphrates: From Foraging to Farming at Abu Hureyra.* London: Oxford University Press.

Smith, M. E., 1973. *Picture Writing from Ancient Southern Mexico: Mixtec Place Signs and Maps.* Norman (OK): University of Oklahoma Press.

Wendorf, F. (ed.), 1968. *The Prehistory of Nubia.* Taos (NM): Fort Burgwin Research Center, distributed by Southern Methodist University Press (Dallas).

Wendorf, F. & Schild, R., 2001–2003. The late Paleolithic burials at Jebel Sahaba: the earliest known warfare. *Scienze dell'Antichità Storia Archeologia Antropologia,* 579–592.

Wendorf, F. & Schild, R., 2004. Late Paleolithic Warfare in Nubia: The Evidence and Causes. *Adumatu,* 7–28.

Willey, G. R. & Phillips, P., 1958. *Method and Theory in American Archaeology.* Chicago (IL): University of Chicago Press.

Yoffee, N. & Sherratt, A., (eds) 1993. *Archaeological Theory: Who Sets the Agenda?* Cambridge: Cambridge University Press.

4

Theory, Fashion, Culture

Mark Pluciennik

There is a certain irony in the fact that the session organisers and contributors to 'The Death of Archaeological Theory?' found so much to say about a potentially deceased or even non-existent corpus – or maybe that is a particularly archaeological speciality. Under the circumstances it seems reasonable to start by asking once more what we mean by archaeological theory – does such a term make sense and is it desirable to expect a coherent and unified set of disciplinary concepts? Given that I suspect that many session contributors had a particular and historical corpus in mind when they dissected – or even celebrated – its demise, I also want to examine the role of 'fashion' in setting archaeological and theoretical agendas, focusing here on parts of the Anglo-American world that are better known to me. I want to suggest that the role of intellectual fashion – that is, what appears particularly appealing because of peer pressure or other circumstances – is understated in terms of its influence on the shape of archaeological 'theory' and may help explain why the contours look as they do today. As a case study I examine particularly a shift in 'paradigm envy' from physics to biology.

What then should or could 'archaeological theory' embrace within its confines? A consensus view might be that 'theory' involves thinking about a particular subject in terms of general or abstract principles, and is particularly concerned with explanation rather than description. However, just as archaeological objects, concepts and entities do not fall into neat, self-evident or uncontested categories, no more do the processes of explanation, understanding and description themselves.

Further, apparently neutral terms themselves have histories and reflect particular ways of thinking about the entities concerned. Hence similar concerns arise if we try to draw dividing lines between archaeological description, method and theory. Nevertheless, theory is particularly concerned with the conceptual frameworks which provide the contexts and enable the meanings of archaeology and its various data, and for that reason often extends into and overlaps with disciplines ranging from anthropology, philosophy, psychology and history to biology, geology, chemistry and physics. If methodology is more about how we might operationalise those ideas through empirical investigation, analysis and synthesis, theory and methodology overlap: both are ultimately ways of considering and applying ideas to archaeological materials and archaeological practices. Certain methodologies may imply or exclude particular theories, and *vice versa*.

Thus the issue of 'theory', when addressed explicitly, has always raised questions about where one might position archaeology as a discipline, and hence what kinds of concepts might be most appropriate. Archaeology is often characterised as straddling the ground between the arts and humanities, on the one hand, and the sciences on the other. These divisions themselves go back to nineteenth-century concerns about whether there were particular methodologies, approaches and degrees of certainty associated with particular types of knowledge. But however one wishes to characterise or place archaeology, it is clear that it is a very broad discipline in terms of the variety of timescales, materials, ideas and techniques it uses to study the human past, and, increasingly and importantly, the uses of the past in the present. It embraces the material (including the biological and textual), the social and the ideational. In what sense and to what degree should an academic archaeologist interested in, say, the meanings of urban spaces in ancient Rome overlap theoretically with one studying human origins? Or the study of colonial effects on settlement patterns impact upon research into Upper Palaeolithic art? Or a professional concerned with site presentation or community archaeology share epistemological or other frameworks with a ceramic analyst? Although there may well be some shared techniques, or understandings regarding material culture, for example, archaeologists working on different topics or undertakings will be posing different kinds of questions in very different contexts, and will typically find different conceptual frameworks appropriate. Archaeology is necessarily multi-, inter- and trans-disciplinary – but rarely in the same ways for different projects or practitioners. Such eclecticism may be seen as excellent and as promoting open-mindedness; the downside is that, even in a relatively small discipline, and with rising numbers of publications, it can lead to divergence, fragmentation and superficiality (Johnson 1999, 182, 187).

Two further preliminary comments: firstly, it is commonly accepted that whatever viewpoint we may adopt *vis-a-vis* constructivism – see for example the exchanges between Hodder (1997, 1998) and Hassan (1997) – we are all 'situated': necessarily the product not only of individual circumstances, but also of broader institutional, cultural, educational, social, economic, political and historical contexts. It is this fact which means that we can expect both diversity and common trends in archaeological and academic thought, certainly within institutions and countries, and often on a wider scale too. However, this diversity – and we should also recognise that archaeological concerns and hence at least implicit theory are not confined to archaeologists – does not mean that we cannot agree about some things. We clearly have many common practices, and hence languages with common terms and concepts through which we can often, though not always, *meaningfully* discuss our similarities and differences (LAW 1997). But secondly, this also implies that there are many ways of relating to, describing and interpreting similar objects, entities or experiences. Hence it also highlights the importance of history and the vagaries of cultural fashion: we pursue, or react against, previous ideas, as well as working within a particular set of constraints and possibilities in any particular place and time. That sociopolitics shape archaeological theory and practice variously in different places at different times, is widely accepted (*e.g.* Kehoe 1998; Patterson 1995; Trigger 1984; 2006). They also suggest new topics and perspectives on the past. One of the most obvious examples of the influence of 'fashion' – present-day concerns – is seen in the recent widespread concern with 'identity' and what it might mean. Current uncertainties in a climate of cultural separatism and pan- or post-national entities have certainly fuelled recent interest in multiple and fluid identities rather than the past certainties of national identity. These and their theoretical attributes and concerns then become transferred into or projected onto the past. Thus one can make a coherent case that the cogency and salience of at least some archaeological theory is a matter of intellectual and other fashion, rather than driven by any internal need. 'Fashion' as commonly understood is also continually changing and innovation necessarily a good, and this also applies to some aspects of archaeological theory. There is within the academic and perhaps other spheres too, an internal economy which tends to valorise the new above 'mere' repetition of method and theory or accumulation of data.

Coherence, eclecticism, dissent

The idea of the 'death of archaeological theory' comes mainly from the world of cultural, particularly literary theory, where the term has been applied particularly to the apparent recent shift away from strongly post-structuralist and deconstructionist positions – what in archaeological circles tends to be bundled together with other recent theoretical stances as 'post-modern' theory. However, the 'post-modern' in archaeology has always been a ragbag: one cannot point to a 'deconstructionist archaeology' in the same way that one might be able to apply the label within literary criticism. Lévi-Strauss, Giddens, Foucault, Althusser, Derrida, Heidegger, Bhabha and Bourdieu for example do not fit very neatly into a single school or theoretical bag. In the literary world, the widespread explosion of interest in (mainly French) thinkers in the last third of the twentieth century has been followed in the 1990s by disaggregation and dissent from that particular programme. Thus Eagleton's *After Theory* begins: 'The golden age of cultural theory is long past' (Eagleton 2003, 1). A related point is made by Hayot (2005), who argues that 'theory' (as opposed to more general 'intellectual work') should be able to 'generate a program', and in this sense theory is rarely if ever done any more. For Leitch (2001, 6) there has been the 'death of theory as a coherent enterprise or field given the recent rise of cultural studies'. He goes on to list 24 sub-fields, including media studies, subaltern studies, leisure studies and gender studies, for instance. 'Each of these sub-fields', says Leitch (2001, 7), 'has a theoretical wing so that theory – along with cultural studies broadly construed – has of late itself undergone significant disorganization'. He also argues (no doubt in a similar way to members of other academic tribes, at least since inter-disciplinarity became not only fashionable but also fundable) that 'literary studies, a more permeable discipline than most, is entangled with history, mythology and religion, psychology, linguistics, philosophy (especially aesthetics), folklore and anthropology, and political economy' among others (Leitch 2001, 8). In cultural studies the inquest into the circumstances surrounding the alleged death, perhaps due to excessive consumption, continues from various viewpoints (*e.g.* Patai & Corral 2005; the 2003 *Critical Inquiry* symposium (*Critical Enquiry* 2004)). One suspects that this particular style of theory was more hegemonic in cultural studies than it ever was in archaeology, though not everyone was wholly convinced at the time either (for example see Callinicos 1989, Norris 1990, 1993; Eagleton 1996). Any 'death of theory' is presumably meant to refer to the demise of a particular French-flavoured confection which I suspect never existed in archaeology: perhaps only Bapty and Yates' (1990) *Archaeology after Structuralism* reflects the peak of a literary-inspired Francophilia. Although archaeology as a discipline has of course been influenced by and taken part in broader cultural movements and theoretical discourses, unlike literary studies, say, it is also strongly constrained by other concerns, namely those related to the empirical and to science.

The birth of archaeological theory

In the recent history of the discipline those in favour of the unity of archaeological theory have generally come from a broadly scientific position: a major driver is the search for certainty of knowledge, and the desire for systematisation enabling, among other things, cross-cultural comparative studies. This was the case in the first explosion of explicit theory in archaeology: that primarily associated with the New Archaeologists of the 1960s and their immediate predecessors. Only in this way, it was argued, could archaeology as a discipline make a fundamental and wide-ranging contribution, rather than offering trivial and localised descriptions of sequences and checklists, which in the American school were often equated to 'history'. The desire to contribute was often associated with an apology for previous bad habits (such as the inappropriate borrowing from other disciplines) displaying a certain lack of confidence. Willey and Sabloff (1974, 131) argue that in the 1940s and 1950s (citing the words of Hoebel) archaeology was seen as extremely limited in its contribution to any broader science of man, 'doomed always to be the lesser part of anthropology'. The result was that 'most archaeologists accepted their marginal position and second-class status with becoming humility'. For others, though, archaeology had to become more systematic, more ambitious, and more scientific. We could point to Taylor (1948), Lesley White – espousing evolution and proposing a new science of 'culturology' (1949) – and Willey and Phillips (1958) as important and influential examples. The funding of archaeology in the United States through the National Science Foundation from the 1950s onwards reinforced this view: as Braidwood (1981, 24) later commented:

> 'I think that in the US at least, the growth of the "new archaeology", with all its scientism, will eventually be understood in part as a response to the growth of the NSF as a source for substantial financial support for archaeology... It was important to behave and talk like a scientist.'

By the time that Binford (1962) wrote his famous 'Archaeology as anthropology' article, discussing how archaeology could further the aims of anthropology, he simply assumed that science was the only game in town. Accepting that anthropology's goals were to 'explicate and explain' human history, he immediately went on to consider 'The meaning which explanation has within a scientific frame of reference' (Binford 1962, 218). Within this paradigm, perhaps of most interest is Binford's notion of 'general theory'. This dealt with 'understanding of the *processes* responsible for change and diversification in the organizational properties of living systems' (Binford 1977, 7 [Original emphasis]). Middle range theory was the way in which such ideas could be evaluated. The language may now seem dated, but nothing here seems to preclude, say, particular social or cultural theories from being included within 'general theory' as part of the 'freedom from nonparadigmatic thought that has perhaps resulted from our little rebellion' (*ibid.*).

Practically and educationally, what has traditionally given 'archaeology' its coherence has been fieldwork (especially excavation) and the material data thus derived: what Binford calls the 'static by-products' of past dynamics. Clarke's equally famous 1973 paper is much more explicit about this. Archaeology is defined as 'the discipline with the theory and practice for the recovery of unobservable hominid behaviour patterns from indirect traces in bad samples' (Clarke 1973, 17). His ideas about the form which a 'comprehensive archaeological general theory' might take is directly linked to and modelled upon the stages involved in excavation (Clarke 1973, 16–17). Although social (and other) theory is mentioned only in passing, in fact it was probably particular forms of socio-cultural theory which produced the most ferment in the subsequent decades of archaeological theory.

But the apparent disciplinary coherence offered by fieldwork is much less convincing today. One reason is because methodological and specialist fragmentation (Jones 2001) together with the dispersal of the 'sites' of and personnel engaged in 'fieldwork' (Pluciennik & Drew 2000; Lucas 2001) has invited other forms of producing coherence and ways of living with divergence (such as the tolerated multi-vocality and plurality typically associated with many major archaeological projects). However other factors have also impinged heavily on the contours of the discipline. In large parts of the American and European domains most excavation is now the remit of private contractors, whose circumstances demand the production of largely descriptive and predominantly empirical reports, rather than time spent on abstract or applied theory or interpretation and synthesis, though with honourable exceptions. The continued rise of historical (here meaning post-medieval) archaeology increasingly includes practices and theoretical concerns which may be closer to social and cultural history (if we want to use these terms) than traditional archaeology. If there is a substitute term which also includes fieldwork then it is probably materiality, but even that may not necessarily be the focus of some who would normally consider themselves to be archaeologists, or who reside in archaeology or North American anthropology departments. The field of material culture studies is often very distant from traditional archaeological concerns. There is a vastly-expanded interest in the sociological and political aspects of the discipline, and with the meanings and implications of heritage and archaeology and its various stakeholders (Joyce 2002; Smith 2004), including public perception and recognition (Holtorf & Drew 2007) and the associated community and public archaeologies.

It may be useful, then, to think of the more abstract or generalising parts of archaeological theory as a way of broadly questioning *why* and *how* we are looking at the archaeological record (itself a controversial term) or defining archaeological practices in the ways that we are. This can also be called 'critical theory' in a loose sense, and certainly both 'new' and 'post-processual' archaeologists produced programmatic statements about what archaeologists *ought* to be doing, and eventually helped to profoundly alter the climate of thought. In this view, the most sustained recent attempt to produce a 'general theory' and programme for action has been a particular version of evolutionary archaeology (see below). Overall theory, of whatever kind, can also be seen as opening up discursive, reflective and practical spaces – ways of pushing against, expanding or redefining the boundaries of the discipline. Sometimes new methodologies and data – whether indigenous to the discipline or imported from elsewhere – can have a similar result: they can force archaeologists to confront or re-confront questions which had either thought to have been answered or put on one side as unanswerable. I would argue that the impact of genetic analyses of modern populations has largely worked in this way: although often couched by geneticists in terms of simple 'answers', their primary value for later prehistory onwards has been to force archaeologists to re-engage with the complexities of the social and cultural processes underlying diffusion and migration, for example.

Envy, aspiration, rhetoric

In understanding why the contents of theory take the trajectory that they do, almost certainly the importance of the search for and pressures to achieve personal and disciplinary status and rewards is underplayed. It has been suggested above that 'science' as an icon and an aspiration played an important role in influencing the direction and language of archaeological theory (*cf.* Tilley 1990, 138–141); in turn this provoked a rhetorical counter-reaction against 'scientism'. Many tended to take 'hard' science and especially an anachronistic idea of a Newtonian physics (*cf.* Massey 1999, 264) as their model of how archaeological methodology and theory should develop, though that certainly did not mean that they were uninterested in social aspects of change; indeed, they often wanted precisely to address these kinds of anthropological questions about social organisation, for example, but through the application of a particular form of scientific reasoning. This shift towards quantitative and often logical positivist approaches was seen elsewhere, in geography and history, for example. Massey (1999) interestingly explored the subsequent shift in emphasis within geographical theory from the 'physics envy' of the former towards more relational philosophies of science which could also encompass the uncertainties of quantum theory, within a discipline which has contained its own broad spectrum of interests by naming a division between physical and human geography. Massey also describes the competition among several disciplines or sub-disciplines to be seen as the 'hardest' in scientific terms, and a sense of inferiority to physics from, for example, geologists and biologists.

Have claims to a 'general theory' gone away then? There have been several suggestions for appropriate models for archaeology or for the past, but, with one exception, these are rarely if ever couched as explicit bids for an exclusive and universal framework. For example, many have drawn inspiration from the differentiated timescales or rhythms expressed by Braudel, and seen contrasts between the *longue durée*, *conjoncture*, and *évenément* as pertinent and stimulating (*e.g.* Bintliff 1991b; Knapp 1992; Barker 1995) for philosophies of history as they relate to regional studies. Candidates from the avowedly 'post-processual' camp and more inclined to social theory might be Foucauldian notions of power; or practice theory in the form of Gidden's structuration and Bourdieu's *habitus*, all referenced extensively over the last twenty years; or associated concerns with agency (Dobres & Robb 2000). But these approaches are generally carefully proposed for particular circumstances (*Annales* approaches are often associated with landscape, survey and environmental data sets, for example; agency theory considered appropriate for certain kinds of questions and not as a panacea). In fact within archaeology (but also within anthropology and occasionally history, as well as what its practiiners call 'evolutionary psychology'), a small number of people have claimed over the past couple of decades that not physics, but biology, and specifically Darwinian evolutionary theory should and must be the exclusive basis for any new theory of archaeology. I am not concerned here with the validity of the arguments (for that see *e.g.* Ingold 2000, Kristiansen 2004, Shennan 2002), but rather wish to point to the particular rhetoric involved. What is clear is that for many of the protagonists, the status once associated with physics now attaches rather to biology and genetics: *this* is how real science should be done; this is what archaeology should aspire to. Here I have deliberately culled quotes from the evangelical extremes of the selectionist field. The argument is often not very subtle but seems to be framed by four main, and not unfamiliar, rhetorical strategies.

The first is to posit ignorance on the non-Darwinian archaeologist's part followed by a description of Darwinian theory.

> 'To gain an appreciation of just how different Darwinism is from other theories about the natural world, once cannot simply read a few books or articles and come away with the requisite understanding. Rather, one needs to wade through myriad epistemological issues ...' (O'Brien & Lyman 1999, 72).

The implication here is, of course, that Darwinian archaeology is not like other approaches which do require reading only 'a few books or articles'; this is a familiar tactic in academic writing, aimed at claiming authority and putting the reader on the back foot. It is generally followed by dense referencing to an unfamiliar body of literature – in this case, rather than French philosophers (Bintliff 1991a), it is biological theory.

The second is simply to assert that because Darwinian theory is accepted elsewhere, it must be applicable to all questions relating to humans and culture:

> 'In fact, there is only one candidate for a background theory on which anthropology can be founded, and that is Darwin's theory of evolution' (Nettle 1997, 284).

> 'Evolutionary Archaeologists are simply seeking to bring, for the first time, the most productive set of rules ever used to understand life on earth to the human past – Darwinian theory' (Leonard 2001, 93).

> 'A successful theory of the social system of one species must show how that system arose from the general principles which govern the social systems of all species (and organic life more generally)' (Nettle 1997, 285).

The third is to claim that since the *capacity* for culture (*i.e.* the human brain) can be said to have evolved, culture itself *must* also be subject to the same rules *i.e.* there are no emergent features. This *may* perhaps be a characteristic of culture, though the reasoning is certainly logically false. However, it is, interestingly, usually put in the sense that to think otherwise is both arrogant and politically incorrect, and sets humans apart from other animals, by exempting them and culture from Darwinian evolution. Thus we are still put in thrall to our biological history (this is, of course, also the line that is adopted by evolutionary psychologists – that our natures are ineradicably determined by our evolutionary history, and 'culture' is not strong enough to overcome our palaeolithic propensities). However the fourth – and perhaps the most pervasive rhetorical claim – is simply that Darwinian theory works in (parts of) the biological sciences; that humans are biological; and that archaeology should comply. In other words, Darwinian theory in one form or another is necessary to gain proper scientific credentials.

> 'There are only two [Darwinian] basic choices and, more fortunately still, either one gives us a general theory *intelligible to natural scientists* and compatible with their general theory' (Bettinger 1991, 221).

> 'For the product [archaeology] to be useful it must adhere faithfully to the central tenets of Darwinian evolutionary theory' (O'Brien & Lyman 2000, 22).

This is all part of the attempt to close off debate and pluralism by demonstrating – in O'Brien and Leonard's own words – 'that Darwinian evolutionism is a superior product to any number of alternatives readily available in the marketplace' (2001, 18).

This argument that we must imitate the natural sciences (but here meaning biology) is simply a revised version of the 'paradigm envy' discussed above. Perhaps archaeology is particularly prone to agonising over its place in the disciplinary scheme of things, simply because it sits at the intersection of scientific and humanistic interests. For selectionists, in the current climate, with the apparent ascent of molecular biologies and genetics in both the public and scientific spheres, Darwinian biological models are preferred. Consider the following quotes (emphases added):

'The most critical issue raised...[is] *[c]an we use the archaeological record to study evolution*, or we restricted simply to studying change?' (O'Brien & Lyman 1999, 73).

This is also a restatement of the prejudice against and misunderstanding of 'history' which was also common to much new archaeology:

"'history" without "science" cannot produce an explanatory account of the past, only a listing of disconnected facts' (Bettinger & Richerson 1996, 222).

Our disciplinary commitment might generally be thought of as exploring the past with whatever theoretical 'tools' appear appropriate, not insisting that the past must fit the tools. But for selectionists:

'Ultimately it is not necessarily the role of science to explain phenomena – archaeological or otherwise – as much as it is to order observable phenomena into a system consistent with our [Darwinian] perception of reality' (O'Brien & Holland 1995, 195).

Thus for many cultural selectionists any questions about human history are not usually derived from instances of the archaeological or historical record; rather they are how to *make* the theory of evolution *applicable* to a suitable portion of the archaeological record. Behind this is the desire to get in on the act with the 'big boys' and current perceptions of 'real' and successful science and its associated funding and status:

'We can, however, take heart in the fact that palaeobiologists, who also deal with a nonliving record, faced just this problem... but eventually were afforded seats at ..."the High Table of evolutionary theory"... [A]rchaeologists can similarly escape the "dead hand of history"' (O'Brien & Lyman 2000, 72).

'An anthropological theory which writes its own ground-rules, incommensurate with those of natural history, [will mean that] anthropology will face a slow retreat before the advance of more realistic disciplines such as history, economics, sociobiology, and evolutionary psychology' (Nettle 1997, 285).

My point here is that insistence on the need to find a grand or general theory has certainly not disappeared. The protagonists are just as fervent in tone as earlier claimants, and if anything more programmatic. 'It is our goal to effect a complete paradigm shift within archaeology, not merely to amuse ourselves with academic debates' (O'Brien & Holland 1995, 193–194). Given that such proposals go back to the 1980s (*e.g.* Dunnell 1989, 44–49), were Darwinian archaeology to become as dominant as its supporters wish, a future historian might see the current apparent disarray as a moment of theoretical reanimation, rather than a death bed scene. But there is a strong argument that such claims about the 'obvious' advantages of a Darwinian or evolutionary archaeology – which have now been made for more than twenty years with little influence on mainstream archaeology – are much more to do with the fashion for things Darwinian, than any superior explanatory value within archaeology.

Death, rebirth, transformation

Despite the above, at present there seems little sign of any widespread or fundamental theoretical shift, though of course such periodisation is often done with hindsight, but rather dispersal of the sites of theory production. Neither should one exaggerate the unity of past periods or 'movements' or the extent to which they represent a rupture with previous practice. Names such as 'Post-processual' or 'New' archaeology often signalled a shift in emphasis, rather than wholesale change. It may even be that selectionist archaeologies eventually do prove to be the fittest and gain greater currency than they have now, and will be seen as marking a shift towards some radically new theoretical paradigm. Nevertheless, two recent publications have addressed the question of the diversity of archaeological theory more broadly. I have argued above that archaeology's chronological extension (up to and including the present) and the incorporation of other interest groups has increased this trend. Hodder, though, argues that methodological, material, period and area specialisms have inevitably meant that a diversity of interests and their associated 'languages' (or terminologies), conferences and journals, for example, is the 'normal' state of affairs in archaeology, as in other disciplines.

> 'We should not then bemoan theoretical diversity in the discipline. Diversity at the current scale may be fairly new in

theoretical domains, but it is not new in the discipline as a whole. These productive tensions are important for the discipline as a whole' (Hodder 2001, 4).

Such productivity though demands, if not direct communication and exchange, at least awareness of variability. Thus Kristian Kristiansen has argued that there is a need for a form of rapprochement and rethinking of the task of archaeology, precisely because rather than a tolerant 'plurality' of approach, contemporary archaeological theory is rather characterised by 'disparity', with 'mutually incompatible traditions that ignore publications aligned with other theoretical programmes' (Kristiansen 2004, 77). The death of theory, if that is what it is, has happened through fragmentation and dispersal of both the sites of theoretical authority and spaces for agreement.

The 'death of theory' in archaeological terms refers to the apparent collapse of a spurious consensus: one should not necessarily confuse visibility or audibility with conventional wisdom or accepted practice. While there may be moments of particular polemic in which it is useful to place oneself or one's work under one rubric or another, one suspects that many archaeologists have a relatively eclectic approach to theory as much as method, in the best sense of the word: that new approaches may stimulate different questions (and *vice versa*). After all, one of the European Association of Archaeologists session organisers has, among other traditions, drawn for inspiration on Annales historians, chaos theory, and Wittgenstein as ways of engaging with materials derived from the Boeotia survey project (Bintliff 1991b; 1997; 2000).

As Shanks (2004, 503) has noted, archaeology can also be thought of as a form of cultural production; as such, we should perhaps expect it to be more fully exposed to the vagaries of fashion – cultural politics – in ways that physics and biology are perhaps not. We could mourn the death of theory; we could celebrate the disorganisation of theory, as the form that theory has now; or we could note that, unsurprisingly, the nature and range of 'theory' is not the same as it was 10 or 20 years ago.

References

Bapty, I. & Yates, T., (eds) 1990. *Archaeology after Structuralism: Post-structuralism and the Practice of Archaeology*. London: Routledge.

Barker, G., 1995. *A Mediterranean Valley: Landscape Archaeology and Annales History in the Biferno Valley*. London: Leicester University Press.

Bettinger, R., 1991. *Hunter-gatherers: Archaeological and Evolutionary Theory*. New York: Plenum Press.

Bettinger, R. & Richerson, P., 1996. The state of evolutionary archaeology: evolutionary correctness, or the search for a common ground. In H. Maschner (ed.), *Darwinian Archaeologies*, 221–232. New York: Plenum Press.

Binford, L. R., 1962. Archaeology as anthropology. *American Antiquity* 28, 217–225.

Binford, L. R., 1977. General introduction. In L. Binford (ed.) *For Theory Building in Archaeology*, 1–10. New York: Academic Press.

Bintliff, J., 1991a. Post-modernism, rhetoric and scholasticism at TAG: the current state of British archaeological theory. *Antiquity* 65, 274–278.

Bintliff, J., (ed.) 1991b. *The Annales School and Archaeology*. Leicester: Leicester University Press.

Bintliff, J., 1997. Catastrophe, chaos and complexity: The death, decay and rebirth of towns from antiquity to today, *Journal of European Archaeology* 5, 67–90

Bintliff, J., 2000. Archaeology and the philosophy of Wittgenstein. In C. Holtorf and H. Karlsson (eds), *Philosophy and Archaeological Practice. Perspectives for the 21st Century*, 153–172. Goteborg: Bricoleur Press.

Braidwood, R., 1981. Archaeological retrospect 2. *Antiquity* 55, 19–26.

Callinicos, A., 1989. *Against Postmodernism*. Cambridge: Polity Press.

Clarke, D., 1973. Archaeology: the loss of innocence. *Antiquity* 47, 6–18.

Critical Enquiry 2004. The Future of Criticism: A *Critical Inquiry* Symposium. *Critical Inquiry* 30 (2), 324–479.

Dobres, M-A. & Robb, J., (eds) 2000. *Agency in Archaeology*. London: Routledge.

Dunnell, R., 1989. Aspects of the application of evolutionary theory in archaeology. In C. Lamberg-Karlovsky (ed.), *Archaeological Thought in America*, 35–49. Cambridge: Cambridge University Press.

Eagleton, T., 1996. *The Illusions of Postmodernism*. Oxford: Blackwell.

Eagleton, T., 2003. *After Theory*. London: Allen Lane.

Hassan, F., 1997. Beyond the surface: comments on Hodder's 'reflexive excavation methodology'. *Antiquity* 71, 1020.

Hayot, E., 2005. The death of theory. *Printculture* (31 October). http:www.printculture.com/item-442.html.

Hodder, I., 1997. 'Always momentary, fluid and flexible': towards a reflexive excavation methodology. *Antiquity* 71, 691–700.

Hodder, I., 1998. Whose rationality? A response to Fekri Hassan. *Antiquity* 72, 213–217.

Hodder, I., 2001. Introduction: a review of contemporary theoretical debates in archaeology. In I. Hodder (ed.), *Archaeological Theory Today*, 1–13. Cambridge: Polity Press.

Holtorf, C. & Drew, Q., 2007. *Archaeology Is a Brand!: The Meaning of Archaeology in Contemporary Popular Culture*. Walnut Creek: Left Coast Press.

Ingold, T., 2000. The poverty of selectionism. *Anthropology Today* 16 (3), 1–2.

Johnson, M., 1999. *Archaeological Theory: An Introduction*. Oxford: Blackwell

Jones, A., 2001. *Archaeological Theory and Scientific Practice*. Cambridge: Cambridge University Press.

Joyce, R., 2002. *The Languages of Archaeology*. Oxford: Blackwell.

Kehoe, A., 1998. *The Land of Prehistory: A Critical History of American Archaeology*. New York: Routledge.

Knapp, B., (ed.) 1992. *Archaeology, Annales and Ethnohistory*. Cambridge: Cambridge University Press.

Kristiansen, K., 2004. Genes versus agents. A discussion of the widening theoretical gap in archaeology. *Archaeological Dialogues* 11 (2), 77–99

LAW (Lampeter Archaeology Workshop) 1997. Relativism, objectivity and the politics of the past. *Archaeological Dialogues* 4 (2), 164–198.

Leitch, V., 2001. Disorganization and death of theory American style. *Hungarian Journal of English and American Studies* 7, 5–9.

Leonard, R. D., 2001. Evolutionary Archaeology. In I. Hodder (ed.), *Archaeological Theory Today*, 65–97. Cambridge: Polity Press.

Lucas, G., 2001. *Critical Approaches to Fieldwork: Contemporary and Historical Archaeological Practice*. London: Routledge.

Massey, D., 1999. Space-time, 'science' and the relationship between physical geography and human geography. *Transactions of the Institute of British Geographers* (NS) 24, 261–276.

Nettle, D., 1997. On the status of methodological individualism. *Current Anthropology* 38 (2), 283–286.

Norris, C., 1990. *What's Wrong with Postmodernism: Critical Theory and the Ends of Philosophy*. Hemel Hempstead: Harvester Wheatsheaf.

Norris, C., 1993. *The Truth about Postmodernism*. Oxford: Blackwell.

O'Brien, M. & Holland, T., 1995. The nature and premise of a selection-based archaeology. In P. Teltser (ed.), *Evolutionary Archaeology: Methodological Issues*, 175–200. Tucson: University of Arizona Press.

O'Brien, M. & Leonard, R., 2001. Style and function: an introduction. In G. Rakita & T. Hurt (eds), *Style and Function: Conceptual Issues in Evolutionary Archaeology*, 1–23. Westport (Conn.): Bergin and Garvey.

O'Brien, M. & Lyman, R., 1999. *Seriation, Stratigraphy, and Index Fossils: The Backbone of Archaeological Dating.* New York: Kluwer Academic/Plenum.

O'Brien, M. & Lyman, R., 2000. *Applying Evolutionary Archaeology: A Systematic Approach.* New York: Kluwer Academic/Plenum.

Patai, D. & Corral, W., 2005. *Theory's Empire: An Anthology of Dissent.* New York: Columbia University Press.

Patterson, T., 1995. *Towards a Social History of Archaeology in the United States.* Fort Worth: Harcourt Brace.

Plucienník, M. & Drew, Q., 2000. 'Only connect': global and local networks, contexts and fieldwork. *Ecumene* 7 (1), 67–104.

Shanks, M., 2004. Archaeology and politics. In J. Bintliff (ed.), *A Companion to Archaeology,* 490–508. Oxford: Blackwell.

Shennan, S., 2002. *Genes, Memes and Human History: Darwinian Archaeology and Cultural Evolution.* London: Thames and Hudson.

Smith, L., 2004. *Archaeological Theory and the Politics of Cultural Heritage.* London: Routledge.

Taylor, W. W., 1948. *A Study of Archeology.* American Anthropological Association Memoir 69. Washington: American Anthropological Association.

Tilley, C., 1990. On modernity and archaeological discourse. In I. Bapty and T. Yates (eds), *Archaeology after Structuralism: Post-structuralism and the Practice of Archaeology,* 128–152. London: Routledge.

Trigger, B., 1984. Alternative archaeologies: nationalist, colonialist, imperialist. Man 19, 355–370.

Trigger, B., 2006. *A History of Archaeological Thought (second edition).* Cambridge: Cambridge University Press.

White, L., 1949. *The Science of Culture: A Study of Man and Civilization.* New York: Grove Press.

Willey, G. & Phillips, P., 1958. *Method and Theory in American Archaeology.* Chicago: University of Chicago Press.

Willey, G. & Sabloff, J., 1974. *A History of American Archaeology.* San Francisco: W. H. Freeman.

5

Theory in Central European Archaeology: dead or alive?

Alexander Gramsch

Invited by John Bintliff and Mark Pearce to contribute to their session on the 'Death of Archaeological Theory?' at the 2006 EAA meeting in Krakow I felt the need to argue from a perspective different from theirs: that of an archaeologist socialised into the German tradition. This tradition is rooted firmly in a distinctive Central European Archaeology. Imagine a German archaeologist talking about the death of theory – would not that be anachronistic? Things obviously are more problematic and tangled where theory in Central European Archaeology is concerned. Thus, this paper will first address the questions what 'Central European Archaeology' is supposed to mean, and how this particular way of doing archaeology is associated with or approaches theory. This, in turn, requires us to talk about what 'theory' does or may mean, and how it is related to practice. I will add some thoughts on reflexive approaches to theory/practice. What are current debates among Central European archaeologists revealing about attitudes towards both 'our real aims' and the methodologies that might be appropriate to achieve them? Before attempting theory's life in Central Europe we should ask: what is it that we ought to kill? Is theory alive at all?

Introduction

For several years now, an increasing number of Central European archaeologists have debated the nature of different archaeological traditions in Europe, their national histories of archaeology and its epistemological backgrounds (*e.g.* papers in Hensel *et al.* 1998; Kobylinski 2001; Biehl *et al.* 2002a). But it will be necessary to go beyond both the histories and the current state of these traditions to understand what an 'archaeology without theory' might mean for these archaeologies. Within a Central European framework the plea for a 'Death of Theory' has a very different meaning compared to the Western European context where it has been developed, and thus has to be approached differently. The questions I will try to answer in this paper concern the attitudes Central European Archaeology takes towards theory and practice. Is it desirable to argue for the death of theory in this particular context? Is theory alive at all?

To answer these questions I have to circumscribe Central European Archaeology (CEA) first, seen both from the angle of the German tradition in which I have been raised and from the experiences I made while comparing theory and practice in archaeology across Europe (Biehl *et al.* 2002a; Gramsch & Sommer forthcoming a). To describe the particular approach of the Central European tradition to theory and its relation to practice I will introduce two German terms: *Materialschlacht* and *Theoriefeindlichkeit*. Here a distinction between archaeological theory and theoretical archaeology will be helpful. Finally I will develop a certain notion of 'reflexivity' to think about recent and future developments of both theory and practice in Central European Archaeology.

Talking about Central European Archaeology

Let me first discuss CEA as one of several major archaeological traditions in Europe. The following definition of these traditions results in particular from a conference held in Poznań in 2000 (Biehl *et al.* 2002a) and a session held at the Esslingen EAA meeting in 2001 (Gramsch & Sommer forthcoming a). The Poznań conference had been organised under the premise that the Iron Curtain could have had a considerable impact on the ways archaeologists in Eastern and in Western Europe communicate and practice archaeology; therefore we entitled it 'Archaeologies East – Archaeologies West'. It became clear, however, that rather than a simple east–west divide, strong West European, Central

European and East European (Russian) archaeological traditions exist that transcend both national borders and academic networks (Biehl *et al.* 2002b).

During the Esslingen session we debated the German influence on other Central European archaeological traditions. We argued for a new understanding of CEA characterised by a particular *habitus* rather than by certain '-isms' different from those in the West and East (Gramsch & Sommer forthcoming b). It is not a lack of 'Processualism', 'Structuralism' or 'Post-processualism' *etc.* that distinguishes CEA from other major traditions – CEA means a particular way of doing archaeology, *i.e.* of dealing with material culture and, moreover, of presenting interpretations to peers, to fellow archaeologists. To elaborate on this a brief sketch of the recent history of archaeology will be necessary.

After the political changes of 1989–90, the countries of the former Soviet dominion were keen to renew the ties to countries of Western Europe. To consolidate these links a cultural kinship was emphasised. This was subsumed under the renewed brand '*Mitteleuropa*' (Central Europe). '*Mitteleuropa*' does not denote a clear-cut geographical region. Rather this vague term signifies an idea, a concept. For example, in 2001 a new culture journal was launched, called *Kafka – Zeitschrift für Mitteleuropa*. It was produced by the Goethe Institut Inter Nationes e.V., and published in Poland, Hungary, Czech Republic, Slovakia, and Germany in their respective languages; it aimed at promoting the 'discourse with and between the Central European culture areas,' as the editors stated in the first issue (Brodersen *et al.* 2001, 5 – my translation). Central Europe today is primarily perceived as the sum of these 'culture areas' ('*Kulturraum*'). '*Mitteleuropa*' always has been a highly politicised concept – however, it is interesting to note that the recent re-evaluation of this concept means a shift from a political and geo-strategical notion, which came to be misused by the Nazis to legitimise their ambitions to dominate their eastern neighbours (Gramsch & Sommer forthcoming b), to an emphasis on a 'community of values', which needs to be preserved and intensified (Brodersen & Dammann 2005, 9).[1]

Archaeology was part of this 'cultural move'. Prehistoric archaeology is understood as part of the humanities and, thus, part of European culture, expressing European values (see Gramsch 2000a). In a number of publications since 1990 archaeologists from Poland, Ukraine, the Czech Republic *etc.* emphasised that throughout history their national archaeological tradition 'was connected with the archaeology of Central Europe' (Lech 1996, 194); and that the 'situation of Polish archaeology ... does not differ from a general picture of archaeology in Central Europe' (Minta-Tworzowska & Rączkowski 1996, 209). During the Poznań and Esslingen conferences they made clear that Marxism did not entirely change both theory and practice but that their respective archaeological schools were still rooted in the common Central European tradition.

Interestingly, they used the label 'culture-historical archaeology' to denote this common tradition: while in other contexts this label may mean an insult, here it signifies common ground. As Predrag Novaković points out, '[t]he tradition of culture history was simply too strong and too deeply rooted to be replaced. [...] the Yugoslav post-war national archaeologies remained deeply rooted in the Central European ('German') culture history paradigm' (Novaković forthcoming; see also Kadrow forthcoming). CEA was expected to be historical, *i.e.* to contribute to national and cultural self-identification, as Sklenář (1983) already pointed out (Novaković 2008, 42).

Central European culture-historical archaeology thus was strongly geared with German archaeology, due to its dominant position as a 'majority tradition', in Evžen Neustupný's words (1997–1998, 2002). In the nineteenth and large parts of the twentieth century the German university system and German language played a major role in education in neighbouring countries. Many Polish, Slovene, Romanian and other archaeologists were trained by German and Austrian teachers (*e.g.* Kadrow forthcoming; Gheorghiu & Schuster 2002). A well-known example is Józef Kostrzewski, who studied archaeology with Kossinna as his tutor and, as professor in Poznań, used the culture-historic paradigm and Kossinist methods to fight German claims to areas that were now Polish (Rączkowski 1996, 203–208; forthcoming). But also others such as Erazm Majewski in Warsaw, and Leon Kozłowski in Lwów followed the culture-historical paradigm of the 1910s and 1920s, with Kozłowski defining culture as characterised by a number of traits such as implements, pottery, burial rites, house form and so on (Lech 1996, 180–183). In Belgrade, Milutin Garašanin was assigned a teaching post in 1958, and '[t]he profound German influence, firmly set in the previous decades of archaeology in Serbia, and still apparent in many parts of Europe at the time, is strongly felt in his work', following Gero von Merhart's comparative typology and Paul Reinecke's chronological system (Babić 2002, 313). Also 'Czech archaeologists were largely influenced by the literature written in German, but they have been moving toward English recently' (Neustupný 2002, 286). From the 1960s onward CEA picked up new trends only partially, and developed a simplified view of Western archaeologies as being overtly theorised and 'post-something'. In general, despite the use of Marxist vocabulary by some central European archaeologists and sometimes declarative citations from the Marxist classics in archaeological writings, the mainstream of archaeology in almost all of these areas was firmly in the culture-history mould (Barford 2002, 83). However, rather than the simple traditional-postprocessual dichotomy, we can observe that CEA developed an alternative academic culture, a *habitus* different from other traditions: teaching and debating (Sommer 2000, 2002a), formulating research questions, practising archaeology *etc.* varied considerably in the distinct research traditions in Western, Central and Eastern Europe.

Materialschlacht vs *Theoriefeindlichkeit*

Let us take a closer look at the *habitus* of CEA: a popular attitude in much of traditional Central European prehistoric archaeology is 'to let the facts speak for themselves'. It is a topos which is frequently used, in particular in publications aiming at the detailed presentation of excavated material. This so-called *Materialschlacht* is a typical feature of traditional prehistoric archaeology in Germany, and also frequent in other Central European archaeologies (though less extensive, see Rączkowski forthcoming). '*Materialschlacht*' actually could be translated as 'material battle', *i.e.* the term was coined to describe a battle strategy exhausting a huge amount of human and material resources, *e.g.* during the Battle of Verdun. In German archaeology it is frequently used to denote, sometimes ironically, large-scale studies, quite often dissertations, which cope with a wealth of archaeological material, mainly artefacts and structures, resulting in extensive catalogues and detailed distribution maps, often at the expense of the interpretation.

On the other hand, for more than two decades now the complaint is regularly lodged about German archaeology's distance or even hostility towards theory (*e.g.* Härke 1983; 1989). Thus '*Theoriefeindlichkeit*', *i.e.* the supposed 'hostility towards theory', is another frequent topos, in particular in German language publications on the history and state of the art of archaeology in Central Europe (*e.g.* Klejn 1993; Härke 1995). These two topoi can be seen as a sort of bracket for the themes I will touch upon next.

Georg Kossack, one of the most prolific and renowned German archaeologists, also used the topos that facts could speak for themselves. Presenting tremendous volumes on the large-scale research project of the development of settlement in coastal regions he set the goal 'die Befunde aus sich heraus zu verstehen' (Kossack *et al.* 1984, 49), thus following the '*Materialschlacht*' attitude. But what lies at the heart of this? Was Kossack a-theoretical or even '*theoriefeindlich*'?

Several years ago John Bintliff (2001) acclaimed Kossack's work for being grounded in a firm theoretical basis without pushing theory to the forefront. Reviewing English translations of a selection of Kossack's work, Bintliff noted that it paralleled the development of processual and post-processual approaches. However, Kossack did not centre on the theoretical background of his approaches – nor did most of the researchers of his generation. Bintliff made two points:

> 'First, the "theory" that underlies Kossack's essays is always understated, and introduced on top of weighty discussion of the 'material', *i.e.* the artefacts or structures each essay focuses on; and second … not a hint can be found that he is interested in what scholars younger than him … are writing about in the UK or the USA' (Bintliff 2001, 284).

This insight also may have triggered Bintliff's demand for the 'Death of Theory' since he concludes:

> 'then how important actually are those packages of theories to the steady advance of progressive analyses of the Old World past?' (Bintliffe 2001, 285).

So could such a material-oriented approach advance progress in archaeology? Let us take a closer look at an example. Of course it is problematic to single out one individual work – it never can represent the whole phenomenon (and such a brief discussion will always do it an injustice). The volume I have chosen indeed is particular in some respect. It is a monograph based on a dissertation submitted at the University of Marburg, and what makes it particular is the fact that it begins with a rather unusually critical chapter on the history of research. This chapter explicitly discusses the nationalist and National Socialist misuse of the excavations and their results which the book publishes.[2] At the same time, this monograph is a typical representative of the *Materialschlacht* approach. Michael Strobel's (2000) *Die Schussenrieder Siedlung Taubried I* sets out to present the late Neolithic settlement 'Taubried I', excavated in 1927 and 1937 in the Federseemoor, a bog in southern Germany which is famous for its well-preserved wooden building structures. Published in a single volume the dissertation comprises 596 pages and 119 plates. The table of contents alone is eight pages. Its main aims are the presentation of the finds and the wooden building structures, and the interpretation of building sequences, construction methods *etc.*, so the largest part discusses features and findings and lists them in detailed catalogues. Also different settlement types are compared regionally, since the questions arise, where the shift from early and middle Neolithic large-scale buildings on dry ground to the clusters of small pile dwellings in wetlands first occurred, and how this innovation was introduced to the Northern Alpine region in the late Neolithic. However, little is said about concepts of culture contact and culture change, let alone the concept of culture itself. Again a wealth of evidence is presented on similar settlements in Lower Austria, Slovakia, and Hungary, discussing their features and dating (Strobel 2000, 306–320), but it is only at the very end of this chapter that we can find thoughts on how these settlement types and construction methods could have developed and, perhaps, spread. Strobel carefully hints at the effect of tradition ('*Traditionsgebundenheit*') and small-scale regional developments (p. 319), as well as at possible western and eastern influences and the culture change obvious in material culture traits (p. 320). Again, he refrains from explicitly discussing whether house and settlement types have been communicated between groups, and whether they represent groups at all. Analysing and comparing changes in pottery shapes and decoration, he concludes that here, too, a clear eastern influence is visible which may be due to population movements (pp. 422–433). In the background we can detect a culture concept that perceives culture traits – house forms and building techniques, pottery shapes and decoration – as representing a set of shared ideas which could have been communicated between different regions. However, while such a normative culture concept and the subsequent migrationist explanations are applied consistently, they are never openly discussed.

Strobel is not only aware of Kossinnist misinterpretations, he is also able to deconstruct them explicitly, but still he follows the traditional mode of presenting, analysing, and interpreting the material. Obviously it is not simply the post-war empiricism, which Günter Smolla (1979–80) characterised as the 'Kossinna syndrome', which distinguishes the German-type *Materialschlacht*-archaeology from Western Archaeologies – and this holds true also for other schools within CEA. Rather than being hostile towards theory (*theoriefeindlich*), post-war scholars such as Kossack and Smolla, Hensel and Tabaczyński did follow model-based research agendas. However, explicit debates about theory have always been avoided, since they were deemed unnecessary to the development of archaeological interpretation. Sławomir Kadrow emphasises that also Polish researchers 'were avoiding theoretical reflections', concentrating on culture-historical archaeology (Kadrow forthcoming).

Thus, the accusation of *Theoriefeindlichkeit* does not tell the full story about the CEA attitude. The years following World War II even saw debates centring on theoretical issues rather than introducing theory through the extensive presentation of archaeological material. The discussions published in Germany in the 1950s concerned new approaches, *e.g.*, to settlement archaeology and cartography (Kahrstedt 1950; Eggers 1951; see also Gramsch 1996; 2003), or to the 'ethnic paradigm' (*e.g.* Eggers 1950).[3] Trying to get free from the Nazi legacy, the issue of archaeology and ideology was also approached (Jacob-Friesen 1950). Jacob-Friesen used the opportunity of a necessary dissociation from any kind of 'dogma' to argue for a positivist attitude: archaeologists should focus on the full strength of pure facts and maintain an 'ideology-free' historical discipline (Jacob-Friesen 1950, 2). Parallel to the institutional reconstruction of prehistoric archaeology a reworking of its contents was sought-after. Moreover, there always have been continual debates about the concept of archaeological cultures, and its relation to ethnic and other identities (*e.g.* Sangmeister 1967, Bergmann 1970, Lüning 1972; see also Veit 1989, Wotzka 1993, and recently

Burmeister & Müller-Scheeßel 2006), and about archaeology's general aims and potentials (Fischer 1987; Veit 1995). These debates reveal the theoretical background of German '*Urgeschichtsforschung*'. However, explicit discussion of this background never became an important part of German mainstream archaeology. And we have to keep in mind that this mainstream to a large degree retained the positivist paradigm.

There is a long tradition of both dealing with theory in a very subtle way and of practising archaeology without explicitly reflecting on its premises and paradigms. Since the late 1950s impressive large-scale projects were launched in Germany (Wolfram 2000), which could not have taken place without a minimum of thought about the hows and whys of archaeology, and which influenced Central European neighbours (Kadrow forthcoming). The difference to other, in particular Western European, archaeologies lies not in the quantity of theory but in the *habitus*. This difference is also visible in teaching: as Ulrike Sommer complains, 'students are taught to be critical about data, not about ideas' (2000, 235).

Although it seems paradoxical, the attitude of CEA (and German archaeology in particular) towards theory was to have no attitude. Thus, CEA for many decades was *theoriefeindlich* in the sense that it was unwilling to reflect upon its historical and social basis and its paradigms – while at the same time theory did exist (Veit 2002, 414).[4] Despite its claimed *Theoriefeindlichkeit*, the absence of or hostility towards theory, even for Central European Archaeology it was impossible to come to interpretations without a theoretical base – however, the *way to cope* with this base was different from both Western and Eastern archaeologies. Until today doing archaeology means above all excavation and classification, it means field archaeology and the ordering of huge amounts of data (*Materialschlacht*). Theory follows practice – or rather: it follows material. In the 1970s and 1980s it was the renewed belief in technical progress[5] that made large-scale excavations a major archaeological practice (Wolfram 2000), since the 1990s it is the rise of scientific archaeology, of archaeobiology and archaeometry, of DNA and isotope analysis, that inspires new research. Interdisciplinary research is perceived as the silver bullet (Atzbach 1998). The background to this attitude is that answering new research questions is a matter of more and 'better' data, not of concepts, premises and paradigms. Still positivism and the twin concepts of evolutionism – describing the development of culture traits – and diffusionism – describing their spread – at large form the basis of CEA theory (Rączkowski forthcoming).

It is important to note that this difference in attitude between Western and Central European archaeologies even became enlarged with the advent of revolutionary paradigm shifts in Anglo-American archaeologies since the 1960s. Manfred Eggert was one of the first to try to introduce the new questions and debates into CEA (*e.g.* Eggert 1978). In Poland, Stanisław Tabaczyński and others referred to some of the questions raised by Lewis Binford and David Clarke (Kadrow forthcoming). In Slovenia, Binford lectured for one semester at the University of Ljubljana in 1985, and soon afterwards courses on archaeological theory appeared in the curriculum (Novaković forthcoming). However, most of the mainstream archaeologists rejected both the questions and, in particular, the style of the debate. The revolutionary attitude in challenging traditional views led to the perception of New Archaeologists as being akin to communists (*cf.* Sommer 2002a). This way of asking new questions and dealing with the research of predecessors was so strange to most Central European archaeologists that they did not even bother to distinguish between theoretical archaeologists as such, processualists, post-processualists *etc.* Funnily enough, however, both North American archaeology and the German school share similar accusations: both are said to display a 'self-imposed isolation' (Kohl 2002, 425) and ignorance towards other, non-majority traditions (Neustupný 2002).

Theoretical archaeology or archaeological theory?

We can conclude that while theory did and does exist in CEA, theoretical archaeology does not. 'Overt theorising' as has been ascribed to Western European archaeologies by Bintliff and Pearce never took place, neither in Germany nor in Central European Archaeology as a whole. Rather, some notable local schools were established – I have mentioned Evžen Neustupný (Prague, now Plzen) and Manfred Eggert (Tübingen). Already since the 1960s some younger scholars felt the need to catch up with the new developments. Increasing in number they founded circles and groups outside of mainstream archaeology, such as the 'Unkeler Kreis' in 1983 (Härke 1983, 1989) and, in 1990, the German Theoretical

Archaeology Group (T-AG) (Theorie-AG 1991; see www.theorieag.de). Both intended to introduce questions and approaches which were felt to be neglected, to create a network of theoretically oriented prehistorians, and to promote theoretical debate which eventually might be able to achieve a paradigm shift. They organised sessions and conferences and included 'theory' into their teaching, and subsequently a number of volumes on 'theory' were published (*e.g.* Wolfram & Sommer 1993, Bernbeck 1997, Härke 2000, Gramsch 2000b, Burmeister & Müller-Scheeßel 2006).

But what does theory mean, after all? Does archaeological theory exist? Or theoretical archaeology? These questions are not new, but they still need to be discussed with vigour. Recently, a session organised by the journal *Archaeological Dialogues* for the 2006 SAA meeting in San Juan focused on this issue. Matthew Johnson in his keynote speech approached the question 'does archaeological theory exist?' and found the Solomonic answer: yes and no. Theory in archaeology does exist, but it cannot be characterised as a distinctive, autonomous body of knowledge (Johnson 2006).

Schiffer (1988) listed three different approaches towards 'theory' in archaeology: a) any concept or consideration applied to a specific explanation of a particular past phenomenon; b) a more reflective level of fundamental assumptions, a paradigm; c) a series of basic premises, postulates or assumptions, often implicating phenomena that are unobservable, such as domestication or Hellenisation. Central European authors use the term 'theory' sometimes with reference to a particular set of *a priori* assumptions linked to a particular research problem, sometimes 'theory' means social theory or Marxist thought or the like, *i.e.* a body of knowledge deriving from other contexts, outside archaeology, that try to explain human behaviour or human action or historical processes in general. But quite often 'theory' is defined negatively and used pejoratively, denoting anything that is not practice (Veit 2002, 414f.).

Traditional culture-historical archaeology tried to maintain its self-characterisation as being empirical, as objective as possible, and free of ideological influences. The reaction to the advancing theory debate in the 1980s and 1990s was that 'theory' was a buzz word imported from 'the Anglo-American' discourse (*e.g.* recently Behrens 2002), and used in an Oedipal manner (see Pearce this volume) by, *e.g.*, Unkel and German T-AG colleagues. This is countered by regular short but pressing appeals to 'discuss theory' and to become free from 'isolation' resulting from empiricism or 'Marxist domination' (*e.g.* Marciniak & Rączkowski 1991; Lech 1997–1998; Härke 1989; Atzbach 1998). Many of the debates of Unkel and German T-AG turned into complaints about the *Theoriefeindlichkeit* of mainstream approaches. For both Western and Central European archaeologists preferring a more explicit use of models and concepts the representatives of the traditional CEA *Materialschlacht* attitude were old-fashioned, and 'the German school' became a pejorative term, misrepresenting the diversity of approaches to theory and practice (Rączkowski forthcoming).

It is important to note here that, as Johnson says, the theorising in Western archaeologies did not lead to a better understanding of the relation between archaeological practice and archaeological thought; rather, he claims, it established a separate theoretical thinking aside from everyday archaeological thinking. He states that 'the relationship between explicit archaeological theory and other elements of archaeological thinking and practice has itself been under-theorized' (Johnson 2006, 120).

We may illustrate this using a parable. The philosopher Ernst Bloch has retold an old Chinese story of three olive eaters. These men of letters met to eat three olives each – however, the case is particular: the olives had been placed into a quail which was stuffed into a duck which was wrapped with a goose placed in a turkey, in a sow, in a sheep, in a calf, and finally in an ox. After roasting all this on a spit the drippy mound of meat was cast away and the olive eaters chewed silently the delicate fruits. After a while one of the men broke the silence: 'I suppose the turkey was not quite young!'

Theoretical archaeologists used to be like these men: trying to meat up the fruit of their labour they wrapped it in ever new, sometimes heavy cloaks of theory – usually without getting rid of the cloak that was already there, but also without properly joining the various theoretical coatings. Simply put: the 'archaeology of ethnos' (culture-history) was not replaced by but rather jacketed by the 'archaeology of process' which again was not replaced by but supplemented by other archaeologies: cognitive, landscape, symbolic and structural, neo-evolutionary *etc.*

Today Bintliff, Pearce and others feel the need to get down to the fruit again: to telling stories about past societies. But this fruit, 'the past', has acquired the flavours of all the different types of theoretical meat, we cannot 'think the past' without thinking of all that we have learned in our academic practice. And what is more important: probably 'the past' would not be digestible without all that we have added. Thus, one preliminary answer to the question what 'theory' is and why we need it simply is that it makes the past digestible, it makes possible to tell stories comprehensible in the present.

Reflexivity

That said we need to talk about how theoretical argument should help – while avoiding 'overt theorising'. Both the above sketch of the *Materialschlacht* attitude of CEA and Matthew Johnson's (2006) analysis of archaeological theory in Western archaeologies show the need for reflexivity: archaeologists of any academic tradition are obliged to reflect about both the nature of our subject and the nature of our thinking. For example, how could a Central European or Western or any other archaeologist approach human history without an awareness of the very different understandings of terms, concepts, models and data they are using?

Rather than arguing for the death of theory I want to argue for reflexive approaches. This requires not to get rid of the 'theoretical archaeologist' but for the practical archaeologist to become a theorist and vice versa. Rather than maintaining the theoretical subdiscipline we have established – also in CEA – I would like to promote the spread of theoretically founded reflexivity into archaeological practice. This reflexive attitude should involve several issues:

Reflection about the history of research

A reflexive historiography of CEA is necessary – not in terms of a teleological account of achievements, but as an epistemological and deconstructive reading of the relations between historic and structural frameworks, *Zeitgeist*, and archaeological thinking and practice. In Germany in particular every PhD thesis and most books begin with a chapter on the history of research ('*Forschungsgeschichte*'); however, rather than analysing the social, political and historical or simply the academic background of research again, a seemingly objectified cataloguing of dates of discoveries and important publications is preferred (as has been said above, Strobel's (2000) deconstruction is exceptional). Not surprisingly these historiographies in fact are not objective, rather they present an apparent inherent logic in the development of research questions and approaches, silencing both the influences and constraints upon research and the alternatives for it. Thus, a reflexive attitude must involve reflection about how and why certain research questions evolved rather than others, and if these questions are formulated and answered *driven by* the present or *relevant for* the present. Reflection therefore also requires us to deconstruct the canonical reading of older publications and to reconstruct the particular context of their emergence (Flaig 2005, 183).

Reflection about archaeology's social role

Today the archaeological disciplines face the challenge to prove their social relevance more than they have done previously. While this is caused by ongoing budget reductions or threats to close down university institutes it nevertheless is a chance to think about what kind of story we want to tell and which message we would like to transmit to 'the public' and how we could achieve this. A recent approach is the analysis of how archaeology is presented and perceived in the media and in schoolbooks (Sommer 2002b; Sénécheau 2003, 2008; Biehl 2005; Samida 2006; Benz & Liedmeier 2007). Moreover, we need to reflect how to avoid the 'identification trap' that has tortured much of CEA: stories of past societies that are of public interest have tended to link past and present through invented traditions, rendering nation or Europe identical to past societies (see Gramsch 2000a, 2005 on 'Europeanism'; for a non-nationalist approach to narrating stories relevant for present societies see Magnusson 2005; see also Kristiansen 2007). Without theoretically informed reflexivity we tend to reproduce particular narratives and to legitimate sectional interests.

Reflection about practice as theory and theory as practice

Today archaeology becomes ever more specialised, integrating a vast array of methods and subjects and approaches such as micromorphology, forensics, underwater research, statistics *etc*. We need to reflect about this development to be able to continue to integrate these approaches and to combine their different strands of thinking. This means understanding theory as a component of archaeological practice and practice as theory-laden, and this understanding requires reflexivity.

There is nothing 'common-sense' about archaeological data; they do not 'speak for themselves'. Reflexivity thus means to scrutinise how we gain our data, on which grounds our interpretations rest and what they reveal beyond the author's intentions. Reflexivity requires us to contextualise archaeological practice socially, politically, economically. This again requires at least a certain quantity of 'theory' (if theory can be quantified) for *all* those thinking and practising archaeology. Behrens (1999) postulated that it would be enough if 10% of archaeologists deal with theory. Of course, the opposite is true: theoretically informed reflection about the hows and whys of all kinds of archaeological practice – excavating, ordering, public presentation *etc*. – is necessary, not only for a handful of theorists spinning in their separate subdiscipline.

The argument for a merging of practice with theory also works the other way round: the reflection about how our data can be used, about how consensus on interpretations emerges, about how our stories are read outside of the academic discourse and so on – this reflection requires us to understand theoretical discourse, interpretation and story-telling *as practice* (recently: Tomášková 2006). To understand the 'practice of theory' we need to step back and reflect.

A luxury nobody can afford?

In his early days the Australian archaeologist Tim Murray was told he was 'a luxury no Archaeology Department could afford' because he was interested so much in both the history and theory of archaeology (Lucas 2007, 158).

Rather, it would be a luxury to do archaeology without theory. Although agreement may never be achieved as to what 'theory' or 'theoretical archaeology' comprise, theory in archaeology is needed to conduct intellectual debate. Tim Schadla-Hall (2004, 256) recently noted that some research questions and interpretations lose their credibility after one or two generations only. To understand this process we need to discuss how much it is driven by new data or by other factors. How and why do some approaches and interpretations gain higher symbolic capital than others? Is the question as to what counts internationally as 'theory' linked to the domination of the English language and the rise of English-language theoretical debates since the 1960s, ignoring older discourses? How much does the credibility of an argument or an interpretation rest upon its appeal to different authorities or different ways of presenting both data and theory? Is it true, as I have indicated, that the low regard for much of CEA in Western archaeologies and the devaluation of the 'German school' results to a large degree from differences in *habitus*?

Death of theory in Central European Archaeology?

In CEA it is not archaeological theory or theorising that obscures our pathways to reconstruct the past but an underdeveloped reflexivity and the bad linkage of theoretical discourse with archaeological practice. In post-war Germany a whole generation failed trying to transform archaeological practice through theory. Rather, German T-AG and others have established a separate discourse, but not even a subdiscipline. But this is nothing to complain about. Bintliff and Pearce asked us to explore alternative approaches to a formal subdiscipline 'Archaeological Theory'. I want to challenge the value of archaeological theory as a subdiscipline, *i.e.* something that some of us do, called archaeological theorists, while others, archaeological practitioners, do archaeology. It cannot be our aim to maintain archaeological theory as a separate discourse, rather we are in need of theory and reflexivity in archaeology as something which gives us the appropriate tools to reflect about what we are doing, what others believe we are doing, what we try to tell about the past and what others understand.

Bintliff's and Pearce's demand to discount the burden of 'dogmatic theory and ideology' thus needs to be reformulated, and it needs to be contextualised. The dogmatic ideology in CEA differs from that of other archaeologies: it says that it is ideology-free, material-centred and oriented towards feasibility. The dogmatic theory also says that there are archaeological facts which speak for themselves, if we only gain more material and properly order and present it. To break free from these dogmas, however, it is not the 'death of theory' which is necessary but more enhanced reflexivity. Theory's importance and relevance is not diminished by the affirmation of the importance of the data in evaluating archaeological arguments (Johnson 2006). Rather, it is increased, because theory is central for enabling us both to turn the collecting and ordering of material into convincing accounts of the past and to reflect the epistemological basis both of our own and of others' archaeologies.

Differences between Western and Central European archaeologies, the Anglo-American and the German traditions in particular, also lie in their self-understanding: while the former was part of anthropology the latter saw itself as the ugly sister of history with underdeveloped links to anthropology and sociology. Questioning the necessity of archaeological theory – or theory in archaeology – requires us to consider these different regional, historical and epistemological contexts to avoid the trap of universalising statements (Tomášková 2006). I agree that it is reasonable to debate, for example, an overuse of phenomenology and agency theories in some discourses. Funnily enough though, a Heideggerian archaeology exists only outside Germany. And it is funny, too, that it was Heidegger who maintained that humans always have a 'pre-theoretical' understanding of the world that is a result of our always already *Being-in* it, *i.e.* a knowledge of the material world as well as of other people resulting from practice. Thus, if you like, we could use this particular understanding of phenomenology to justify the traditional Central European mode of subordinating theory to practice. But we can also use it to justify the maintenance of a reflexive attitude which ought to enable us to analyse this 'pre-theoretical' knowledge underlying our practice.

So the question if we shall kill theory – if not the theorists – has to be answered according to the various contexts of theory production and application, not surprisingly: killing theory in CEA may have a conservative and reactionary effect. Considering production and consumption contexts has to be part of a reflexive attitude as much as the debate about what Bintliff and Pearce call 'our real aims' and the debate about the stories we want to tell.

Theory and reflexivity, are thus needed to participate actively in the uses for which archaeological information is put – 'we must not stand by and let people misuse it for whatever horrendous political capital they want to make out of it', as Tim Murray recently put it (Lucas 2007, 166). And referring to the Kossinna-syndrome he continued: 'when you're building it [theory], remember that it's not a game, and you owe a duty of care to people, to be as clear as possible about what you're doing and about the consequences of what happens' (Lucas 2007, 167).

We need to be careful: to avoid overt theorising which loses touch with the empirical basis; to avoid swinging back too far from theoretical debate into the empirical, and starting bean-counting again; and to avoid killing the delicate plant of reflexivity which is growing in various archaeological contexts – not throwing the baby out with the bathwater is the advice I would like to give. Do not be afraid of 'death *by* theory'!

Acknowledgements

I owe much to the discussions with Ulrike Sommer and our joint preparation of the Esslingen conference volume; many of the points raised here result from this. I also would like to thank Peter F. Biehl and Arek Marciniak for our work on the Poznań conference volume and subsequent discussions. This paper would not have been possible without these two conferences, and I am also indebted to their participants. Thanks also to Michael Dietler for valuable comments, and finally to Mark Pearce and John Bintliff for inviting me to present this paper at their EAA session and to publish it in this collection.

Notes

1 According to the editors of 'Kafka' this intensification of common values requires a new and augmented 'European public' – meaning both people and awareness – thus arguing for their own journal which at that time no longer received public financial support (Brodersen & Dammann 2005).

2 Space does not allow me to go into detail here, but let me briefly mention that the infamous Hans Reinerth played a prominent role in the excavations in the Federseemoor and promoted the excavation of the entire site of Taubried I in 1937 (Strobel 2000, 45–52; see also Schöbel 2002, Hassmann 2000).

3   Immediately after World War II it was important for Eggers to emphasise
    that archaeological evidence is not similar to that of ethnology (*i.e.* cultural
    anthropology) and thus does not allow ethnic ascription: 'Archäologischer
    Fundstoff läßt sich also in keiner Weise etwa auf eine Stufe mit der dem
    Völkerkunde und der Volkskunde stellen' (Eggers 1950, 54).

4   '"Theoriefeindlichkeit" bezeichnet ja nichts anderes als jene Abneigung,
    die Bedingungen archäologischen Forschens reflektierend zu erkunden...
    Dies widerspricht nicht der wichtigen Erkenntnis, dass auch in solchen
    "theoriefeindlichen" Bereichen der Forschung implizite Theoriebestände wirksam
    sind' (Veit 2002, 414).

5   A dominant topic for the Western world at that time was technical development
    and how to export this to the less developed countries of what was then called the
    Third World. This also influenced archaeological thought (Rieckhoff 2007).

References

Atzbach, R., 1998. Vom Nutzen und Nachteil der Archäologie. Ein Aufruf zur
    Theoriediskussion. *Archäologisches Nachrichtenblatt* 3, 3–5.

Babić, S., 2002. Still innocent after all these years? Sketches for a social history
    of archaeology in Serbia. In Biehl *et al.* 2002a, 309–321.

Barford. P. M., 2002. East is East and West is West? Power and paradigm in
    European archaeology. In Biehl *et al.* 2002a, 77–97.

Behrens, H., 1999. *Grundfragen der deutschen Urgeschichtswissenschaft. Wo stehen
    die Archäologen am Ende des 20. Jahrhunderts?* Weißbach: Beier & Beran.

Behrens, H., 2002. Was ist mit Theorie gemeint? Ein Zauberwort der Welt-
    Archäologie. *Archäologisches Nachrichtenblatt* 7, 205–209.

Benz, M. & A. K. Liedmeier, 2007. Archaeology and the German press. In
    T. A. R. Clack & M. Brittain (eds), *Archaeology and the Media*, 153–173.
    Walnut Creek: Left Coast Press.

Bergmann, J., 1970. *Die ältere Bronzezeit Nordwestdeutschlands. Neue Methoden
    zur ethnischen und historischen Interpretation urgeschichtlicher Quellen.*
    Marburg: Elwert.

Bernbeck, R., 1997. *Theorien in der Archäologie.* Tübingen & Basel: Francke.

Biehl, P. F., 2005. 'Archäologie multimedial': Potential und Gefahren der
    Popularisierung in der Archäologie. *Archäologisches Nachrichtenblatt* 10,
    240–252.

Biehl, P. F., Gramsch, A. & Marciniak, A., (eds) 2002a. *Archaeologies of Europe.
    History, Methods, Theories.* Tübinger Archäologische Taschenbücher vol. 3.
    Münster: Waxmann.

Biehl, P. F., Gramsch, A. & Marciniak, A., 2002b. Archaeologies of Europe:
    Histories and identities. An introduction. In Biehl *et al.* 2002a, 25–32.

Bintliff, J., 2001. Review of B. Hänsel & A. Harding (eds), Towards translating the past. Georg Kossack – selected studies in archaeology. Ten essays written from the year 1974 to 1997 (Rahden/Westf.: M. Leidorf, 1998). *European Journal of Archaeology* 4(2), 284–285.

Brodersen, I. & Dammann, R., 2005. Editorial: Starthilfe für Europa. *Kafka. Zeitschrift für Mitteleuropa* 16, 8–9.

Brodersen, I., Dammann, R. & Sötje, P., 2001. Editorial: Europa neu entwerfen. *Kafka. Zeitschrift für Mitteleuropa* 1, 4–6.

Burmeister, S. & Müller-Scheeßel, N., (eds) 2006. *Soziale Gruppen – kulturelle Grenzen. Die Interpretation sozialer Identitäten in der Prähistorischen Archäologie.* Tübinger Archäologische Taschenbücher vol. 5. Münster: Waxmann.

Eggers, H. J., 1950. Das Problem der ethnischen Deutung in der Frühgeschichte. In H. Kirchner (ed.), *Ur- und Frühgeschichte als historische Wissenschaft. Festschrift Ernst Wahle,* 49–59. Heidelberg: Winter.

Eggers, H. J., 1951. Die vergleichende geographisch-kartographische Methode in der Urgeschichtsforschung. *Archaeologia Geographica* 1, 1–3.

Eggert, M. K. H., 1978. Prähistorische Archäologie und Ethnologie. Studien zur amerikanischen New Archaeology. *Prähistorische Zeitschrift* 53, 6–164.

Fischer, U., 1987. Zur Ratio der prähistorischen Archäologie. *Germania* 65, 175–195.

Flaig, E., 2005. Die verfehlte Nation. Warum Mommsens Rom nicht ans geschichtliche Ziel gelangte. In A. Demandt, A. Goltz & H. Schlange-Schönhagen (eds), *Theodor Mommsen: Wissenschaft und Politik im 19. Jahrhundert,* 181–200. Berlin: W. de Gruyter.

Gheorghiu, D. & Schuster, C. F., 2002. The avatars of a paradigm: A short history of Romanian archaeology. In Biehl *et al.* 2002a, 289–301.

Gramsch, A., 1996. Landscape Archaeology: of making and seeing. *Journal of European Archaeology* 4, 19–38.

Gramsch, A., 2000a. 'Reflexiveness' in Archaeology, Nationalism and Europeanism. *Archaeological Dialogues* 7 (1), 4–19.

Gramsch, A., (ed.) 2000b. *Vergleichen als archäologische Methode. Analogien in den Archäologien – mit Beiträgen einer Tagung der Arbeitsgemeinschaft Theorie (T-AG) und einer Kommentierten Bibliographie.* British Archaeological Reports International Series 825. Oxford: Archaeopress.

Gramsch, A., 2003. Landschaftsarchäologie – ein fachgeschichtlicher Überblick und ein theoretisches Konzept. In J. Kunow & J. Müller (eds), *Landschaftsarchäologie und geographische Informationssysteme: Prognosekarten, Besiedlungsdynamik und prähistorische Raumordnungen. The Archaeology of Landscapes and Geographic Information Systems: Predictive Maps, Settle-ment Dynamics and Space and Territory in Prehistory. Int. Coll. 15.–19. October 2001 Wünsdorf, Land Brandenburg* 35–50. Archäoprognose I/ Forschungen zur Archäologie im Land Brandenburg 8. Wünsdorf:

Brandenburgisches Landesamt für Denkmalpflege und Archäologisches Landesmuseum.

Gramsch, A., 2005. Archäologie und post-nationale Identitätssuche. *Archäologisches Nachrichtenblatt* 20, 185–193.

Gramsch, A. & Sommer, U., (eds) forthcoming a. *A History of Central European Archaeology. Theory, Methods, and Politics.* Budapest: Archaeolingua.

Gramsch, A. & Sommer, U., forthcoming b. German Archaeology in Context. An Introduction to History and Present of Central European Archaeology. In Gramsch & Sommer forthcoming a.

Hassmann, H., 2000. Archaeology in the 'Third Reich', in *Archaeology, Ideology and Society: The German Experience*, 65–139. Frankfurt am Main: Peter Lang.

Hänsel, B. & Harding, A., (eds) 1998. *Towards Translating the Past. Georg Kossack – Selected Studies in Archaeology. Ten Essays Written from the Year 1974 to 1997.* Rahden (Westfalen): M. Leidorf.

Härke, H., (ed.) 1983. *Archäologie und Kulturgeschichte. Symposium zu Zielvorstellungen in der deutschen Archäologie.* Kiel: Unkeler Kreis.

Härke, H., 1989. The Unkel symposia: The beginnings of a debate in West German archaeology? *Current Anthropology* 30, 406–410.

Härke, H., 1995. 'The hun is a methodical chap': Reflections on the German tradition of pre- and proto-history. In P. Ucko (ed.), *Theory in Archaeology. A World Perspective*, 46–60. London & New York: Routledge,.

Härke, H., (ed.) 2000. *Archaeology, Ideology and Society. The German Experience.* Frankfurt am Main: Peter Lang.

Hensel, W., Tabaczyński, S. & Urbańczyk, P., (eds) 1998. *Theory and Practice of Archaeological Research. Vol. III: Dialogue with the Data: the archaeology of complex societies and its context in the '90s.* Warsaw: Institute of Archaeology and Ethnology, Polish Academy of Sciences.

Jacob-Friesen, K. H., 1950. Archäologie und Weltanschauung. *Die Kunde–Neue Folge* 1–2.

Johnson, M. H., 2007. On the nature of archaeological theory and theoretical archaeology. *Archaeological Dialogues* 14(1), 117–132.

Kadrow, S., forthcoming. The German influence on Polish archaeology. In Gramsch & Sommer forthcoming a.

Kahrstedt, U., 1950. Grundsätzliches zu historischen und archäologischen Grenzen. In H. Kirchner (ed.) *Ur- und Frühgeschichte als historische Wissenschaft. Festschrift Ernst Wahle*, 60–62. Heidelberg: Winter.

Klejn, L. S., 1993. Is German archaeology atheoretical? Comments on Georg Kossack, Prehistoric archaeology in Germany: its history and current situation. *Norwegian Archaeological Review* 26, 49–54.

Kobylinski, Z., 2001. *Quo vadis archaeologia? Whither European Archaeology in the 21st Century.* Warsaw: Institute of Archaeology and Ethnology, Polish Academy of Sciences.

Kohl, P. L., 2002. Advances in archaeology. Comments on 'Archaeologies of Europe. History, Methods and Theories'. In Biehl *et al.* 2002a, 425–429.

Kossack, G., Behre K.-E. & Schmid, P., (eds) 1984. *Archäologische und naturwissenschaftliche Untersuchungen an ländlichen und frühstädtischen Siedlungen im deutschen Küstengebiet vom 5. Jahrhundert bis zum 11. Jahrhundert n. Chr.*, vol. 1. Weinheim: Acta humaniore.

Kristiansen, K., 2007. Do we need the 'archaeology of Europe'? *Archaeological Dialogues* 15(1), 5–25.

Lech, J., 1996. A short history of Polish archaeology. *World Archaeological Bulletin* 8, 177–195.

Lech, J., 1997–1998. Between captivity and freedom: Polish archaeology in the 20th century. *Archaeologia Polona* 35–36, 25–222.

Lucas, G., 2007. Visions of Archaeology: An Interview with Tim Murray. *Archaeological Dialogues* 14(2), 155–177.

Lüning, J., 1972. Zum Kulturbegriff im Neolithikum. *Prähistorische Zeitschrift* 47, 145–173.

Magnusson, Å., 2005. An agenda for the renewal of Swedish heritage management. *Archäologisches Nachrichtenblatt* 10, 194–198.

Marciniak, A. & Rączkowski, W., 1991. The development of archaeological theory in Poland under conditions of isolation. *World Archaeological Bulletin* 5, 57–65.

Minta-Tworzowska, D. & Rączkowski, W., 1996. Theoretical traditions in contemporary Polish archaeology. *World Archaeological Bulletin* 8, 196–209.

Neustupný, E., 1997–1998. Mainstreams and minorities in archaeology. *Archaeologia Polona* 35–36, 13–24.

Neustupný, E., 2002. Czech archaeology at the turn of the millennium. In Biehl *et al.* 2002a, 283–287.

Novaković, P., 2008. Experiences from the margins. *Archaeological Dialogues* 15(1), 36–45.

Novaković, P., forthcoming. The 'German School' and its influence on the national archaeologies of Western Balkans. In P. Mason, B. Migotti & B. Nadbath (eds), *Jubilejni zbornik ob 60. obletnici Bojana Djurića (Bojan Djurić 60th Anniversary Miscellany)*. Monografije Centra za preventivno arheologijo 1. Ljubljana: Zavod za varstvo kulturne dediščine Slovenije.

Rączkowski, W., 1996. 'Drang nach Westen'?: Polish archaeology and national identity. In M. Díaz-Andreu & T. Champion (eds), *Nationalism and Archaeology in Europe*, 189–217. London: University College London.

Rączkowski, W., forthcoming. The 'German school of archaeology' in its Central European context: sinful thoughts. In Gramsch & Sommer forthcoming a.

Rieckhoff, S., 2007. Keltische Vergangenheit: Erzählung, Metapher, Stereotyp. Überlegungen zu einer Methodologie der archäologischen Historiografie.

In St. Burmeister, H. Derks & J. von Richthofen (eds), *Zweiundvierzig. Festschrift für Michael Gebühr*, 15–34. Internat. Arch. – Studia honoraria vol. 25. Rahden (Westfalen): Verlag Marie Leidorf.

Samida, S., 2006. *Wissenschaftskommunikation im Internet: Neue Medien in der Archäologie.* München: R. Fischer.

Sangmeister, E., 1967. Methoden der Urgeschichtswissenschaft. *Saeculum* 18, 199–244.

Schadla-Hall, T., 2004. The comforts of unreason. The importance and relevance of alternative archaeology. In N. Merriman (ed.), *Public Archaeology*, 255–271. London: Routledge.

Schiffer, M. B., 1988. The structure of archaeological theory. *American Antiquity* 43, 461–485.

Schöbel, G., 2002. Hans Reinerth: Forscher – NS-Funktionär – Museumsleiter. In A. Leube (ed.) *Prähistorie und Nationalsozialismus: Die mittel- und osteuropäische Ur- und Frühgeschichtsforschung in den Jahren 1933–1945*, 321–396. Heidelberg: Synchron.

Sénécheau, M., 2003. Zur Rezeption archäologischer Ausstellungen in Schulbüchern und anderen didaktischen Medien. *Archäologische Informationen* 26, 93–109.

Sénécheau, M. 2008. *Archäologie im Schulbuch. Themen der Ur- und Frühgeschichte im Spannungsfeld zwischen Lehrplanforderungen, Fachdiskussion und populären Geschichtsvorstellungen.* Schulbücher, Unterrichtsfilme, Kinder- und Jugendliteratur, Bd. 1, Freiburg. Online-Resource: http://www.freidok.uni-freiburg.de/volltexte/6142/.

Sklenář, K., 1983. *Archaeology in Central Europe. The First 500 Years.* Leicester: Leicester University Press.

Smolla, G., 1979–80. Das Kossinna-Syndrom. *Fundberichte aus Hessen* 19–20, 1–9.

Sommer, U., 2000. The teaching of archaeology in West Germany. In Härke 2000, 202–239.

Sommer, U., 2002a. Deutscher Sonderweg oder gehemmte Entwicklung? Einige Bemerkungen zu momentanen Entwicklungen der deutschen Archäologie. In Biehl *et al.* 2002a, 185–196.

Sommer, U., 2002b. Die Darstellung der Vorgeschichte in sächsischen Geschichtsbüchern des 19. Jahrhunderts. In H.-W. Wollersheim, H.-M. Moderow & C. Friedrich (eds), *Die Rolle von Schulbüchern für Identifikationsprozesse in historischer Perspektive*, 133–160. Leipzig: Leipziger Universitätsverlag.

Strobel, M., 2000. *Die Schussenrieder Siedlung Taubried I (Bad Buchau, Kr. Biberach). Ein Beitrag zu den Siedlungsstrukturen und zur Chronologie des frühen und mittleren Jungneolithikums in Oberschwaben.* Stuttgart: Theiss.

Theorie-AG 1991. Eine neue Arbeitsgemeinschaft: Die Theorie-AG. *Archäologische Informationen* 14(1), 103–105.

Tomášková, S., 2006. On being heard. Theory as an archaeological practice. *Archaeological Dialogues* 13(2), 163–167.

Veit, U., 1989. Ethnic concepts in German prehistory. A case study on the relationship between cultural identity and archaeological objectivity. In S. J. Shennan (ed.), *Archaeological Approaches to Cultural Identity*, 35–56. London: Routledge.

Veit, U., 1995. Zwischen Geschichte und Anthropologie. Überlegungen zur historischen, sozialen und kognitiven Identität der Ur- und Frühgeschichtswissenschaft. *Ethnographisch-Archäologische Zeitschrift* 36, 137–143.

Veit, U., 2002. Wissenschaftsgeschichte, Theoriedebatte und Politik: Ur- und Frühgeschichtliche Archäologie in Europa am Beginn des dritten Jahrtausends. In Biehl *et al.* 2002a, 405–419.

Wolfram, S., 2000. 'Vorsprung durch Technik' or 'Kossinna Syndrome'? Archaeological theory and social context in post-war West Germany. In Härke 2000, 180–201.

Wolfram, S. & Sommer, U., (eds) 1993. *Die Macht der Vergangenheit – Wer macht Vergangenheit? Archäologie und Politik*. Beiträge zur Ur- und Frühgeschichte Mitteleuropas vol. 3. Wilkau-Hasslau: Beier & Beran.

Wotzka, H. P., 1993. Zum traditionellen Kulturbegriff in der Prähistorischen Archäologie. *Paideuma* 39, 25–44.

6

Theory Does Not Die
it Changes Direction

Kristian Kristiansen

o That's the point → Archaeology nowadays is much
more public & important than before → less elitist →

Theory is part of a wider ideological discourse, defined by the academic
and social life of its practitioners. Therefore theory cannot die, but it
can change direction and its role and relative importance may change
in the process. Therefore, what should interest us are the conditions for
such changes, which I shall discuss and briefly exemplify.

One of the most insightful discussions of how changing theoretical
concepts relates to changing academic and ideological interests is Eric
Wolf's last book: *Envisioning power*. Here he set out to analyse the
relationship between culture and power. He criticises social anthropology
for its disinterest in power, at the expense of the symbolic and social
constitution of culture. For Wolf material culture and its strong
symbolic messages is a key to understanding those historical instances
where cultural ideas were mobilised to repress other people and their
cultures. His cases include the Aztecs and National Socialist Germany.
However, as an introduction he presents a history of ideas, a *tour de
force* in the competing theoretical concepts for understanding ideas of
power. According to Wolf: 'Tracing out a history of our concepts can
also make us aware of the extent to which they incorporate intellectual
and political efforts that still reverberate in the present' (Wolf 1999, 22).
He sees the original debate between the Enlightenment and its enemies
to have formed all subsequent debates. Or in his own words:

the problem is that is lacking confidence and it is
saling itself very cheap to governments

'Each encounter provoked reactions that later informed the position taken during the next turn. The issue of Reason against Custom and Tradition was raised by the protagonists of the Enlightenment against their adversaries, the advocates of what Isaiah Berlin called the Counter-Enlightenment. In the wake of this debate Marx and Engels transformed the arguments advanced by both sides into a revolutionary critique of the society that had given rise to both positions. The arguments put forward by this succession of critics in turn unleashed a reaction against all universalizing schemes, schemes that envisioned a general movement of transcendence for humankind. This particularism was directed against Newtonian physics, Darwinian biology, Hegelian megahistory, and Marxian critique, on the debatable premise that they all subjugated the human world to some ultimate teleological goal' (Wolf 1999, 22).

This brief reference to the nineteenth century debate entails all the major ingredients of later debates, including Processual and Post-processual archaeology, and it corresponds to what I have characterised as the changing cycle of Rationalism and Romanticism in archaeological theory (Kristiansen 1996, 1998, fig. 14). John Bintliff has argued along similar lines, although he would trace to Antiquity the origin of these two competing perceptions of the world – the 'Modern' (Rationalism), and the 'Post-modern' (Romanticism) (Bintliff 1993, 2008, fig. 10.1).

However, it does not explain how and why changes take place when we move from one discourse to the next.

In the following I will therefore discuss the specific relationships that exist between theory, method and interdisciplinary borrowing in a historical perspective, because it is crucial for understanding how and why theory changes.

In a study of the 'Birth of Ecological Archaeology' in Denmark over a 150 year period I observed some recurring interdisciplinary correlations between periods of innovation and periods of consolidation in the study of the Neolithisation process (Kristiansen 2001). I summarise them below:

Periods of innovation	*Periods of consolidation*
High natural science impact	Low natural science impact
New natural science knowledge	Traditional natural science knowledge
International research network	National research network
Global problematic	Local problematic

Periods of innovation were generally short, and two such globally innovating periods could be defined, which preceded a rationalistic cycle: from 1850–1860, and from 1940–1950. The first period saw the formation of modern geology, biology/zoology (Darwin, *The Origin of Species* 1859) and archaeology (the definition of the Stone Age), and these achievements were in part the result of interdisciplinary cooperation and inspiration between the main actors at the time, whether they worked in France, England or Denmark. It had been preceded by the publication in English of Thomsen's three-age system (Ellesmere 1848) and Sven Nilsson's evolutionary history of Mankind, which were widely read internationally. Soon a systematic typological approach inspired by biology, was applied to archaeology, exemplified in the work of Oscar Montelius.

The second period saw the development of modern pollen analysis and its application in the reconstruction of vegetation history, the invention of ^{14}C, which revolutionised archaeological dating, and preceded the global use of nuclear energy. Social evolution and economic approaches soon dominated archaeological research, exemplified by Grahame Clark and Gordon Childe, and the new chronologies were employed by Colin Renfrew to forward a new European prehistory based on internal social evolution.

The question now poses itself: are we at a similar moment in time, where new natural science based innovations pave the way for new global knowledge and interpretations? Before we can attempt to answer this question we must analyse some of the dominant trends in archaeological research during the last 25 years, in order to determine archaeology's position in the present post-processual cycle.

A survey of archaeological journals makes it clear that the last 25 years has seen a preoccupation with interpretative strategies linked to individual sites and local areas, from which generalisations were deduced but rarely properly analysed. This trend is demonstrated in Figure 6.1. During the same period methodological rigour declined, as

Antiquity

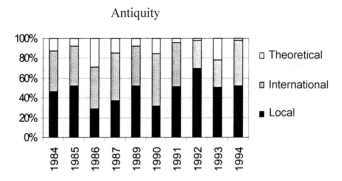

Polona

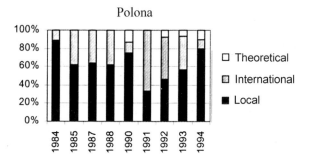

Fontes

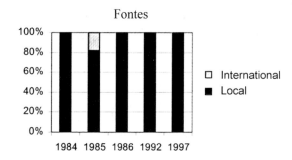

*Fig. 6.1. Analysis of three journals, one international (*Antiquity*), one national with international scope (*Archaeologia Polona*), and one regional (*Fontes*). The articles were divided according to research perspective and analysed at intervals between 1984 and 1997. It demonstrates the strong impact of local presentations even in international journals, and the limited role of theory.*

the need to overlook and analyse large quantities of data declined, just as quantification was considered a processual obsession not needed in the hermeneutic understanding and mediating of data.

The post-processual focus on context has provided many new interpretative perspectives at the local level and in understanding individual sites, which has turned out to be useful also in cultural heritage and public presentations. During the same period archaeological heritage experienced one of its biggest expansions ever and this may have influenced the interpretative concern with local contexts and individual sites in research. A final, but ignored consequence of this narrowing of the interpretative field, is the decline in knowledge outside one's own region or nation. This is demonstrated in Figure 6.2. Especially large nations such as Germany, France and England, with international

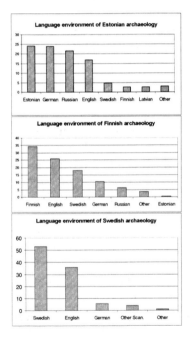
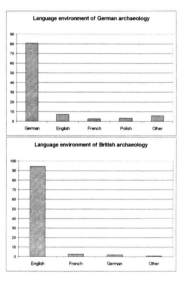

Fig. 6.2. Language analysis of references in leading archaeological journals in Germany and England (large languages) compared to Sweden, Finland, and Estonia (small languages). Source: Lang 2000.

language claims, have tended to become monolingual in their readings and references, while smaller countries such as the Scandinavian, demonstrate familiarity with more languages and readings outside their own borders (Kristiansen 2002).

We may summarise the dominant factors at work during the last 25 years in the following way:

- Dominance of a local perspective/site perspective in interpretation.
- Decline in readings outside one's own language and national borders.
- Expansion of archaeological heritage management and of nationalism. YES !

From this we may conclude that archaeology has strengthened its national position at the expense of its international position, with some exceptions, such as Palaeolithic research. Are these factors related? I believe so: it is no mere coincidence that the local and national focus has dominated theoretical perspectives, heritage and much national politics during the same period. It is a consequence of the humanities' role as critical interpreters of the present that historical disciplines are also following suit. However, the narrowing of the interpretative space to local and regional studies has left archaeology in a weaker position in TOTALLY two important respects: it has lost in academic prestige and subsequently in political support. This is exemplified in the global decline of museum-based research at the expense of public presentation. It corresponds to a period where archaeology abstained from using museum collections for systematic research, but rather employed new excavations, which was also the departure point for reconstructing prehistoric environments that took over much of the role in public presentation during this period. Thus, popularisation expanded in numerous new ways while at the same time academic prestige declined.

The reason for this loss of scientific credibility, I suggest, is that archaeology and the humanities in general have abstained from the big questions that concern most people such as the relationship between climate, culture and environment, which demands grand historical narratives. It may be no coincidence that the two most debated and best-selling archaeological books during the last decade were written by a biologist: Jared Diamond, and dealt with just these questions (Diamond

1997/99, 2005). Other big questions of the present are those of migrations and warfare, which are now slowly entering the archaeological research agenda, or the relation between culture and biology, which has been dominated by evolutionary biologists. Archaeology may be more popular than ever before in the media (Holtorf 2007), and may have achieved an economic foundation of rescue excavations that never existed before the 1970s, but at the same time it has increasingly left some of the big questions to natural scientists, although some archaeologists are taking up the debate and proposing a new agenda. Childe's revolutions may be on their way back, though in revised form (Gamble 2007; Mithen 2003; Renfrew 2007). I propose that these tendencies are the first signs of a retreat from the present post-modern and post-processual cycle towards a more science based, rationalistic cycle of revived modernity.

Thus, there is much to suggest that recent innovations in DNA analysis, strontium isotope analysis, and climate research, are about to change the focus and the direction of much archaeological research towards larger more global problems, even when studied in a local or regional context. I also predict that supra-national, regional studies in tandem with larger historical narratives will become more popular in the future, supported by a more systematic use of analytical and quantitative methods. Mobility and migration as well as ethnicity and warfare will dominate this research. In his new edition of *A History of Archaeological Thought*, Bruce Trigger devoted one of the final chapters to discussing the future direction of archaeological theory, and predicted a period of 'theoretical pragmatism, characterised by an expansion of the theoretical and methodological repertoire', and referred among others to *The Rise of Bronze Age Society* (Kristiansen & Larsson 2005) as an example of this new approach (Trigger 2006, chapter 10, also Flannery 2006).

So my answer to the question if theory is about to die is: no, but it is about to change direction. Whether or not such a change supports the present paradigm by expanding its boundaries or whether it paves the way for a major change of direction only time will show.

GLOBAL TOTAL ARCHAEOLOGY → how incredible
amount of data → what we do with

References

Bintliff, J. L., 1993. Why Indiana Jones is Smarter than the Post-Processualists. *Norwegian Archaeological Review* 26, 91–100.

Bintliff, J. L., 2008. History and Continental Approaches. In R. A. Bentley & H. D. Maschner (eds), *Handbook of Archaeological Theories*, 147–164. Lanham (New York): Altamira Press.

Darwin, C., 1859. *On the Origin of Species by Means of Natural Selection or the Preservation of Favoured Races in the Struggle for Life*. London: John Murray.

Diamond, J., 1997/99. *Guns, Germs, and Steel. The Fate of Human Societies*. New York & London: Norton & Company.

Diamond, J., 2005. *Collapse. How Societies Choose to Fail or Survive*. Penguin Books.

Ellesmere, The Earl of [Francis Egerton], 1848. *Guide to Northern archaeology by the Royal Society of Northern Antiquaries of Copenhagen*. London: Bain.

Flannery, K. V., 2006. On the Resilience of Anthropological Archaeology. *Annual Review of Anthropology* 35, 1–13.

Gamble, C., 2007. *Origins and Revolutions. Human Identity in Earliest Prehistory*. Cambridge: Cambridge University Press.

Holtorf, C., 2006. *Archaeology is a Brand! The Meaning of Archaeology in Contemporary Popular Culture*. Oxford: Archaeopress.

Kristiansen, K., 1996. Old Boundaries and New Frontiers. Reflections on the Identity of Archaeology. *Current Swedish Archaeology* 4, 103–122.

Kristiansen, K., 1998. *Europe before History*. Cambridge: Cambridge University Press.

Kristiansen, K., 2001. Borders of ignorance: research communities and language. In Z. Kobylinski (ed.), *Quo vadis archaeologia? Whither European Archaeology in the 21st century?*, 38–44. Warsaw: Polish Academy of Science.

Kristiansen, K., 2002. The Birth of Ecological Archaeology in Denmark: history and research environments 1850–2000. In A. Fischer & K. Kristiansen (eds), *The Neolithisation of Denmark. 150 Years of Debate*, 11–31. Sheffield: J.R. Collis.

Kristiansen, K. & Larsson, T. B., 2005. *The Rise of Bronze Age Society: travels, transmissions and transformations*. Cambridge: Cambridge University Press.

Lang, W., 2000. Archaeology and language. *Fennoscandia archaeologica* XVII, 103–111. Helsinki.

Mithen, S. J., 2003. *After the Ice: a global human history, 20,000–5000 BC*. London: Weidenfeld & Nicholson.

Renfrew, C., 2007. *Prehistory. The Making of the Human Mind*. London: Weidenfeld & Nicholson.

Trigger, B. G., 2006. *A History of Archaeological Thought*. Second edition. Cambridge: Cambridge University Press.

Wolf, E., 1999. *Envisioning Power. Ideologies of Dominance and Crisis*. Berkeley & London: University of California Press.

7

Have Rumours of the 'Death of Theory' been Exaggerated?

Mark Pearce

....

My purpose in this short contribution is not to cast judgement on any particular (past) theoretical movement or standpoint, but to look to the future, to ask what is the emerging paradigm in this fascinating field of enquiry. I shall argue that the most striking thing about the present state of archaeological theory is that there is no *emerging paradigm to be discerned. I shall propose that Theory is not dead, but has instead become* bricolage *(sensu Lévi-Strauss 1966: 16–22).*

Despite David Clarke's manifesto that 'archaeology is archaeology is archaeology' (1978, 11), I do not think that it would be contentious to say that throughout the post-war period theoretical advances in archaeology have tended to come not from within the discipline, but from other disciplines, such as anthropology, geography or ecology. The Post-processualists, for example, have looked to literary theory for many ideas and approaches. In as much as that theoretical paradigm may be regarded as dominant in archaeology, at least in United Kingdom universities, it is therefore perhaps illuminating to start my paper by looking at the health of 'theory' in literary criticism, with the proviso that in English studies theory has a different meaning than in archaeology, one that is generally limited to denoting post-modern or Marxist approaches to texts. Some workers, such as Mark Bauerlein (1997), have gone so far as to proclaim the *death* of theory in that field.

It would be easy to dismiss such a position as simply reactionary, but I believe that it is instructive to look at the general opinion of the workers in the field of English studies. In 2005, the British university-sector weekly newspaper, the *Times Higher Education Supplement*, conducted a survey of staff in United Kingdom university departments of English; there were 167 respondents. Most (78%) believed that the various 'types of literary theory that have emerged since the 1960s ... have made a positive contribution to the humanities' but, perhaps more interestingly, 44% of respondents thought that the influence of theory was waning in UK universities (*Times Higher Education Supplement*, 7 October 2005; available at http://www.timeshighereducation.co.uk/story.asp?sectionco de=26&storycode=198936; accessed 14 June 2008).

So much for our colleagues in English studies, but what is the situation in archaeology, which borrowed so many aspects of Post-processualism from literary theory? Before answering this important question – which is implicit in the somewhat provocative title, 'Death of theory?', that John Bintliff and I gave to the 2006 Krakow EAA session – I should like to explore a few aspects of the history of theoretical reflection in archaeology. The conventional view of the development of theory in the discipline portrays it as a series of 'paradigm shifts' (see for example Sterud 1973; also Trigger 1981, 152, but *contra* Trigger 2006, 6–9), a view based on Thomas Kuhn's (1970) seminal work, *The Structure of Scientific Revolutions*. It is certainly the case that the protagonists of the New Archaeology presented their work as revolutionary (see, for example, Binford 1972, 1–19, 125–134) and indeed invoked Kuhn's ideas (Binford 1972, 244–245; *cf.* Sterud 1973; Dyson 1993, 203); for Wylie (2002, 21) 'the New Archaeologists demanded no less than a Kuhnian revolution', though we may note that they explicitly rejected Kuhn's view of science (Binford 1983, 233; *cf.* Wylie 2002, 20–21). Whether or not we choose to agree with them, it is clear that the New Archaeology had a transformative effect on the archaeology of many scientific communities (see for example the 'Comments' on Watson's 1991 *Current Anthropology* piece, 'What the New Archaeology has accomplished').

In Bruce Trigger's (1981) outline of the history of archaeology and Gordon Willey and Jeremy Sabloff's (1974, 195) *A History of American Archaeology*, which follow a Kuhnian model of paradigm shifts, the processual revolution was preceded by an empiricist paradigm, the culture-historical approach. Post-processualists would then add a further scientific revolution, ushering in a new paradigm. Not all workers, however, would accept this position, particularly in North America, where the impact of Post-processual archaeology has been less marked.

When I teach this model, this conventional history of archaeological thought, to my undergraduate theory class, I am regularly asked an obvious question: the students note that the New Archaeology came along in the 1960s, to be followed about twenty years later in the 1980s by Post-processual archaeology; more than twenty years have now passed – but what, they ask, is the emerging paradigm?

Now before I attempt to answer this very pertinent question, it might be instructive to think of this twenty-year cycle in a slightly different way. In fact, it could be argued that these 'paradigm shifts' are nothing more than Oedipal murders of academic 'fathers', where theory is used as a weapon against the 'old guard' to facilitate the emergence of a new academic generation (Coudart 1999, 163–164; *cf.* Dyson 1993, 196 for a similar point): thus the processualism of the 1960s was instrumental in furthering the careers of Binford and his associates, before their paradigm was in turn replaced by Post-processualism in the 1980s. This reading is in fact implicit in Binford's portrayal of James Griffin, his teacher at the University of Michigan, as a father-figure in his autobiographical explanations of the background to his early papers (see especially Binford 1972, 125–132; *cf.* 192; indeed, the volume itself is dedicated to Griffin).

But what has emerged or is emerging twenty years after the Post-processualist movement as the next generation seeks its place in the sun, what is their paradigm and who are the new gurus? It is my contention that although the time is now ripe for a 'paradigm shift' to facilitate the emergence of the next generation of archaeological theorists, and a number of theoretical positions have emerged, such as a renewed interest in evolutionary perspectives (see Pluciennik and Kristiansen, in this collection of papers), a new consensus has yet to emerge in our discipline. So why is there no new paradigm? Is it perhaps just that the multiple strands of post-processual theory present a moving target which is so indefinable as to be difficult to pin down and attack?

Part of the problem may be in the perhaps over-facile application of the Kuhnian model to the history of theoretical reflection in archaeology, indeed the history of science has moved on since he published the first version of *The Structure of Scientific Revolutions* in 1962 (*e.g.* Pickering 2001). But because of its widespread use in the history of archaeology, I should like to dedicate some space to analysing Kuhn's model of paradigm shifts, or to 'deconstructing it', to borrow a phrase from our colleagues in literary theory.

Although the succession from culture-historical to processualist to post-processualist which I have outlined may (perhaps) apply to British university archaeologists, it certainly does *not* apply on the continent of Europe, where different archaeological communities have their own theoretical approaches and histories of archaeological thought – this point is well brought out for example by Alexander Gramsch in this collection of papers, and I see no reason to repeat his arguments. Indeed it does not even apply to British university archaeologists, where researchers working in a processual, even in an empiricist culture-historical paradigm, are not very hard to find. Some fifteen years ago Julian Thomas calculated that of the two hundred or so archaeologists in academic positions whom he counted, about half were 'traditional', forty were Processualist, thirty were working in traditions such as Marxism and feminism, whilst probably fewer than fifteen could be classified as Post-processualists (Thomas 1995, 349–351). Whilst generational renewal due to retirements and the expansion of the teaching of archaeology in British universities has probably modified these proportions, they indicate that the 'scientific community' which is central to Kuhn's (1970) model does not really exist, not even in UK archaeology. Nor indeed, *pace* Kuhn, are scientific communities 'necessary features of science as such' (Pickering 2001, 505).

The scientific revolutions story-line is a discourse that favours 'great men' like Binford and Renfrew, or Hodder, Shanks and Tilley, presented as the protagonists and indeed initiators of scientific revolutions, or paradigm shifts (*e.g.* Kuhn 1970, 89–90, 119, 122–123, 125, 144). Rather than by revolutions, it might be argued that scientific development also sometimes proceeds in the incremental, 'building block' way which Kuhn rejected. For example Pickering (2001, 502–503) sees no Kuhnian revolution in the history of particle physics. If we try to see the progress of archaeological thought more incrementally, as based on debate and a plurality of positions, then we begin to discern that rather than ideological adherence to new paradigms, the approach of individual archaeologists is in fact much more nuanced: we tend to negotiate, to vary our position according to the type of question we are addressing, and to chose the method of analysis that fits the problem. And this phenomenon is not just limited to archaeology: for example, mixed methods research, which transcends the conflicts between proponents of quantitative and qualitative research, is emerging as an important research paradigm in a range of social sciences (Johnson & Onwuegbuzie 2004; Tashakkori & Teddlie 2003).

At the risk of being accused of self-obsession I should like to illustrate my point concerning the nuanced, negotiated nature of archaeologists' positions from my own experience. In 1999 I published a paper with an Italian colleague, Armando De Guio (Pearce & De Guio 1999). De Guio is a member of the so-called Padua School of Processualism (Guidi 1996, 31–32): by no means can he be described as a post-processsualist. In our paper we presented a model to explain why in the later Bronze Age, copper ore was transported for smelting to the high Lavarone-Vezzena-Luserna plateau of the Trentino region of northern Italy, far from the outcrops at which it was mined (Pearce & De Guio 1999; see also Pearce 2007, 76–81). I expected that our article would be controversial, not least as it unfashionably posited the existence of a Bronze Age market economy in northern Italy, but I was convinced that its concern with economy and rational market-driven behaviour gave it a clear theoretical stance.

The volume in which the paper appeared, the proceedings of an important conference edited by Philippe Della Casa, was then reviewed in the pages of the *European Journal of Archaeology*; imagine my surprise when I found our article described as 'post-processualist' (Valde-Novak 2002, 133)! Now, whatever the merits of that review or its author's grasp of theoretical viewpoints, what interests me is that the reviewer could perceive of our article in that way. Indeed, rereading what we wrote, I must admit that it is neither wholly processual nor culture-historical, and its language is at the very least influenced by post-processual, or more broadly, symbolic and structuralist, discourse. What that reviewer did not identify was an eclectic, nuanced approach.

Indeed John Bintliff (1993, 98–99; 1995, 32; but especially 2004, xviii–xix) has argued for an 'eclectic approach' to archaeological theory, following Ludwig Wittgenstein's concept of 'complementary discourses'; he tells us that 'A good way to see the eclectic archaeologist faced with the current variety of ways of seeing the past is Wittgenstein's image of the craftsman going out on a job with a large bag of tools – each ideally suited to a particular application within the remit of the profession' (Bintliff 2004, xix). I prefer another metaphor, that of the restaurant: we should move from a *table d'hôte* menu, a fixed theoretical bill of fare, to an *à la carte* approach to theory where archaeologists (diners) choose what is good to think (eat) – which theoretical dish they will try, and which they will eschew. This approach might also be termed *bricolage*, *sensu* Lévi-Strauss (1966, 16–22). That is to say, we should not look for a monolithic paradigm but instead adopt a multiverse (*sensu* Tosi & Pearce 1998) of ways of seeing the past, what in some social science disciplines is called 'mixed methods research' (Johnson & Onwuegbuzie 2004; Tashakkori & Teddlie 2003). Such an approach is attractive because it allows us to select the most effective tools and models and combine them, and it probably represents the actual practice of most archaeologists, although it might be argued that it lacks intellectual rigour. YES - it does

Indeed an eclectic approach, defined by *Webster's Third New International Dictionary* (1966, 719) as 'selecting what appears to be best or true in various and diverse doctrines or methods: rejecting a single, unitary, and exclusive interpretation, doctrine, or method …' seems to be common sense, and its rejection of a single absolutist model seems a soft, reasonable, version of post-modern relativism. There are however two serious objections. The first is that this common sense smacks of 'bourgeois empiricism' (though Trigger [1981, 138] ironically noted that this might be seen as praise by British archaeologists); Johnson and Onwuegbuzie (2004, 16–17, *cf.* tables 1 & 2) make a virtue of this. They argue that pragmatism (in the sense of 'choose the combination or mixture of methods and procedures that works best for answering your research questions') 'can help to build bridges between conflicting philosophies' (Johnson & Onwuegbuzie 2004, 17). The second objection is more serious: we should be aware that in some disciplines, 'eclectic' can be a term of reproach – thus for example some art critics see eclecticism as showing a lack of intellectual rigour, a lack of a coherent approach, or a lack of originality (Mahon 1953): essentially second-rate! It is perhaps of interest that the term 'eclectic' was first used in 1763 by Johann Winckelmann, one of the founding fathers of Classical Archaeology (Schnapp 1996, 258–266), to describe the work of the Carracci (Mahon 1953, 305). This is not just an issue of nomenclature – we could easily use another term than 'eclectic' to describe the approach. Indeed Johnson and Onwuegbuzie (2003, 17) admit that in social science mixed methods research is not 'currently in a position to provide perfect solutions' '… to the metaphysical, epistemological, axiological (*e.g.*, ethical, normative), and methodological differences between the purist positions'. Instead they believe that it should 'use a method and philosophy that attempt to fit together the insights provided by qualitative and quantitative research into a workable solution' and advocate pragmatism as providing this for mixed methods research.

Kuhn (1970, 103–110, 148–150) argues that scientific paradigms are 'incommensurable' in that they lack a common basis of comparison. Bintliff (1993, 99; 2004, xviii) makes the same point about Wittgenstein's 'complementary discourses', that they are not commensurable – that is to say any contribution to our understanding is best evaluated in its own terms, so that for example we cannot assess a post-processual interpretation in processual terms (or *vice-versa*) (though VanPool and VanPool (1999) would disagree with this). Interestingly, if we recast this observation in conventional post-processual terms, eclecticism might be deemed to constitute a multivocal hermeneutic approach (*sensu* Hodder 1991) where the contribution of each theoretical approach is interpreted contextually, and the emerging picture fed into the hermeneutic circle of our understanding of the past as a whole in a 'reflexive' way. I have tried to take such an eclectic approach in my recent work (Pearce 2007).

We might add that much intellectual debate, especially in archaeology, is posturing, and that theoretical positions are not necessarily as different as they appear. A similar observation is made by Kristian Kristiansen and Thomas Larsson in their (2005) book, *The Rise of Bronze Age Society*; commenting on two papers which appeared in the *Journal of European Archaeology*, by Patrice Brun (1995) and Michael Dietler (1995), they note that 'in the debate different levels of explanation are taken to represent different theoretical approaches, leading to a polemic which tends to obscure the legitimacy of both approaches' (Kristiansen & Larsson 2005, 7, note 2). This seems to me to be a very perceptive comment about much theoretical debate in Archaeology, and strengthens the hand of those who would argue for an eclectic approach – why not use elements of both explanatory models, if they are just different levels of explanation? In the second edition of his *A History of Archaeological Thought*, Trigger (2006, 580–581) comments that Kristiansen and Larsson's (2005) book is the 'most extensive, empirically-based effort to transcend the dichotomy between processual and postprocessual … approaches'.

In conclusion, there is no new grand theoretical paradigm emerging accompanied by attendant gurus. I would argue that most archaeologists habitually follow an eclectic (mixed methods) approach in their work, cherry-picking the most effective tools and models and applying them at different levels of interpretation. But if this is the future direction of archaeological theory, then the next paradigm shift, to return to Kuhn's terms, might be the truly revolutionary concept that theoretical paradigms are like dinosaurs – inflexible and useless, and that the future lies in a truly eclectic, theoretically open, approach to interpreting archaeological phenomena. The rumours of the 'Death of Theory' have indeed been exaggerated: theory is not dead, it is just more pragmatic, less partisan, more open – it has become *bricolage*.

Acknowledgements

I am grateful to Hamish Forbes (Nottingham), John Bintliff (Leiden), Torill Christine Lindstrøm (Bergen), and John Robb (Cambridge) for their observations on my contribution; its final form is entirely my responsibility.

[handwritten annotation: It is true, but it could lead to some nihilism, just de-constructionism → better looking for Global Total Arch with the functionality → social role / Saving lifes.]

References

Bauerlein, M., 1997. *Literary Criticism: an autopsy*. Philadelphia: University of Pennsylvania Press.

Binford, L. R., 1972. *An Archaeological Perspective*. New York & London: Seminar Press.

Binford, L. R., 1983, *In Pursuit of the Past. Decoding the Archaeological Record*, London: Thames and Hudson.

Bintliff, J., 1993. Why Indiana Jones is smarter than the Post-Processualists. *Norwegian Archaeological Review* 26 (2), 91–100.

Bintliff, J., 1995. 'Whither archaeology' revisited. In M. Kuna & N. Venclová (eds), *Whither Archaeology?: papers in honour of Evžen Neustupný*, 24–35. Prague: Institute of Archaeology.

Bintliff, J., 2004. Introduction. In J. Bintliff (ed.), *A Companion to Archaeology*, xvii–xxiv. Oxford: Blackwell.

Brun, P., 1995. Contacts entre colons et indigènes au milieu du Ier millénaire av. J.-C. en Europe. *Journal of European Archaeology* 3 (2), 113–123.

Clarke, D. L., 1978. *Analytical Archaeology*. second edition. revised by R. Chapman. London: Methuen.

Coudart, A., 1999. Is post-processualism bound to happen everywhere? The French case. *Antiquity* 73 (279), 161–167.

Dietler, M., 1995. The cup of Gyptis: rethinking the colonial encounters in early-Iron-Age western Europe and the relevance of world-systems models. *Journal of European Archaeology* 3 (2), 89–111.

Dyson, S. L., 1993. From New to New Age Archaeology: archaeological theory and classical archaeology – a 1990s perspective. *American Journal of Archaeology* 97 (2), 195–206.

Guidi, A., 1996. Processual and post-processual trends in Italian archaeology. In A. Bietti, A. Cazzella, I. Johnson & A. Voorrips (eds), *Theoretical and Methodological Problems*, 29–36. Colloquia of the XIII International Congress of Prehistoric and Protohistoric Sciences, Forlì (Italia) 8–14 September 1996, 1. Forlì: A.B.A.C.O.

Hodder, I., 1991. Interpretive archaeology and its role. *American Antiquity* 56 (1), 7–18.

Johnson, R. B. & Onwuegbuzie, A. J., 2004. Mixed methods research: a research paradigm whose time has come. *Educational Researcher* 33 (7), 14–26.

Kristansen, K. & Larsson, T. B. 2005. *The Rise of Bronze Age Society: travels, transmissions and transformations*. Cambridge: Cambridge University Press.

Kuhn, T. S., 1970. *The Structure of Scientific Revolutions*. Second edition, enlarged. Chicago: University of Chicago Press.

Lévi-Strauss, C., 1966. *The Savage Mind (La pensée sauvage)*. London: Weidenfield and Nicholson.

Mahon, D., 1953. Eclecticism and the Carracci: further reflections on the validity of a label. *Journal of the Warburg and Courtauld Institutes* 16 (3–4), 303–341.

Pearce, M., 2007. *Bright Blades and Red Metal: essays on north Italian prehistoric metalwork*. London: Accordia Research Institute (Specialist Studies on Italy 14).

Pearce, M. & De Guio, A., 1999. Between the mountains and the plain: an integrated metals production and circulation system in later Bronze Age north-eastern Italy. In P. Della Casa (ed.), *Prehistoric Alpine Environment, Society, and Economy. Papers of the International Colloquium PAESE 1997 in Zurich*, 289–293. Universitätsforschungen zur prähistorischen Archäologie 55. Bonn: Rudolf Habelt.

Pickering, A., 2001. Reading the *Structure. Perspectives on Science* 9 (4), 499–510.

Schnapp, A., 1996. *The Discovery of the Past: the origins of archaeology*. London: British Museum Press.

Sterud, G., 1973. A paradigmatic view of prehistory. In C. Renfrew (ed.), *The Explanation of Culture Change: models in prehistory*, 3–17. London: Duckworth.

Tashakkori, A. & Teddlie, C., (eds) 2003. *Handbook of Mixed Methods in Social & Behavioral Research*. Thousand Oaks, California/London: SAGE Publications.

Thomas, J., 1995. Where are we now? Archaeological theory in the 1990s. In P. J. Ucko (ed.), *Theory in Archaeology: a world perspective*, 343–362. London: Routledge.

Tosi, M. & Pearce, M., 1998. Introduction. From the Atlantic to the Urals and beyond: the many dimensions of Archaeology. In M. Pearce & M. Tosi (eds), *Papers from the EAA Third Annual Meeting at Ravenna 1997: Volume I: Pre- and Protohistory*, V. British Archaeological Report S717. Oxford: Archaeopress.

Trigger, B., 1981. Anglo-American archaeology. *World Archaeology* 13 (2), 138–155.

Trigger, B. G., 2006. *A History of Archaeological Thought*. Second edition. Cambridge: Cambridge University Press.

Valde-Novak, P., 2002. Review of P. Della Casa (ed)., *Prehistoric Alpine Environment, Society, and Economy: Papers of the International Colloquium PAESE '97 in Zürich. European Journal of Archaeology* 5 (1), 130–133.

VanPool, C. S. & VanPool, T. L., 1999. The scientific nature of postprocessualism. *American Antiquity* 64 (1), 33–53.

Watson, R. A., 1991. What the New Archaeology has accomplished. *Current Anthropology* 32 (3), 275–291.

Webster's Third New International Dictionary of the English Language. Chicago: Encyclopaedia Britannica, 1966.

Willey, G. R. & Sabloff, J. A., 1974. *A History of American Archaeology*. London: Thames & Hudson.

Wylie, A., 2002. *Thinking from Things: essays in the philosophy of archaeology*. Ewing (NJ): University of California Press.